ISAK DINESEN'S AESTHETICS

Kennikat Press
National University Publications
Series in Literary Criticism

General Editor
Eugene Goodheart
Professor of Literature, Massachusetts Institute of Technology

THOMAS R. WHISSEN

ISAK DINESEN'S AESTHETICS

839
813
BLIXEN

National University Publications
KENNIKAT PRESS • 1973
Port Washington, N.Y. • London

Library of Congress Catalog Card No.: 73-83272
ISBN: 0-8046-9059-6

Manufactured in the United States of America

Published by
Kennikat Press, Inc.
Port Washington, N.Y./London

To Anni

CONTENTS

ISAK DINESEN'S AESTHETICS

I
SUBMISSION

ABBREVIATIONS USED FOR BOOK TITLES

SGT *Seven Gothic Tales*
WT *Winter's Tales*
LT *Last Tales*
AD *Anecdotes of Destiny*

1

THE GLORIOUS AMATEUR

ANYONE WHO reads Isak Dinesen's tales soon becomes aware of the presence in all of them of a keen aesthetic sensibility at work. Like the romantic storytellers whom she resembles, she is preoccupied with the processes of artistic creation; and those tales of hers which do not treat of these processes directly do so by inescapable implication. It is in these direct and indirect statements which pervade her tales that I have attempted to find a consistent pattern which could be organized into a total theory of aesthetics.

The study that follows is the result of that investigation. It will do more than offer insight into her own creative imagination and, thereby, her art; it will, I think, provide some stimulating approaches to the eternal questions concerning the act of creation, the product of creation, and the way in which we respond to the created product.

Aesthetics has to do with the creation, communication, and apprehension of beauty; and it is probably obvious that no one of these can be decently appreciated without attention to the others. Like any serious artist, Isak Dinesen pays careful attention to all three. Ignorance of the interrelationships among these three areas of aesthetics signifies, for her, a serious deficiency in at least one of them. I feel that Isak Dinesen was constantly concerned with this ignorance because she saw it accounting for a misunderstanding not just of her own art but of all art. Her comments on aesthetics become, therefore, not only ways of helping the reader through her own works but also ways of making him comfortable in the only world in which we really live—the world of art.

Isak Dinesen never intended to be a writer. She always felt that she was meant for something else entirely, and the seventeen years immediately preceding her first serious literary efforts were spent running a coffee plantation in Kenya, living the sort of life she thought she was destined to live. But destiny, as she was to say herself repeatedly, has more than one role for us to play. When the African adventure collapsed, Isak Dinesen learned to accept her fate; and that acceptance led to the acceptance of her remarkably different role as a writer of exotic tales. From plantation mistress to Scheherazade is a bold step, but it is the step from Karen Blixen to Isak Dinesen, and it is one of the clues to her aesthetic intuition.

Hannah Arendt has pointed out that the first part of Isak Dinesen's life, that part that ended with the collapse of the farm in Africa and her return to Denmark, prepared her for the second part, that part as a writer, by teaching her the lesson of submission.[1] The earlier part is characterized by attempts to impose her own will upon her life; the second part, by a yielding to what she preferred to call "destiny." Others have dealt with this attitude as it affects the theme of her works and as it qualifies as a philosophy, but it is germane to this study in the way that it pertains to her concept of herself as an artist and of the artist in general.

Curtis Cate says of Isak Dinesen that she is "someone who could never be accused of literary professionalism, but who has always been an unseeded player, a gifted outsider, a glorious amateur."[2] What Cate probably means by professional

---

1. "Isak Dinesen: 1885–1962," *The New Yorker* (9 November 1968), p. 236.
2. "Isak Dinesen: The Scheherazade of Our Times," *Cornhill Magazine* (Winter 1959–1960), p. 121.

is the skilled craftsman who has painstakingly learned his art like a trade and whose artistic endeavors are salted not ungenerously with the taint of commercialism. By amateur—the unseeded player, the gifted outsider—he no doubt means the natural artist whose unschooled talent is instinctive and concerned almost solely with expressing itself uninhibited by matters of success or reward.

Isak Dinesen would agree in general with this distinction, I think, but I believe she would define professional and amateur somewhat differently. As we shall see later, Isak Dinesen abhors the self-appointed artist, the one who thinks himself an artist whether he really is one or not. It is this deliberate designation of oneself as an artist that I think she would call professional. In contrast to him is the amateur. He is, as I think she sees him, the artist who is chosen by a will greater than his own. He is the one who willingly submits to his destiny and discovers himself appointed to a role which he may or may not have anticipated—and which he may or may not have wanted. In fact, he is never absolutely certain that he is not deceiving himself. This element of doubt seems to be an essential ingredient of the amateur. Isak Dinesen apparently never lost it even though she felt her career as a writer was not entirely of her own choosing. At any rate, "glorious amateur" is a fitting term for her because she had a natural, unschooled talent and because it is the quality of "amateur" that she prizes most in her concept of the artist.

The idea of a "glorious amateur" is a romantic notion, and in keeping with the romantic tradition, Isak Dinesen feels free to use art and artists as the subject matter of many of her tales. The romantic artist is particularly sensitive to reader response and terribly concerned that the reader should understand something about what an artist does and why he does it. This defensiveness manifests itself in a definite pattern in the four volumes of tales that Isak Dinesen published during the thirty years of her writing life. To begin with, her works show an increasing concern with directing the reader's attention. *Seven Gothic Tales,* her first volume, was considered something of a curiosity, especially in Denmark, and this reception may account for the concern she displays in *Winter's Tales,* her next volume, for the writer who is having doubts about what he has done and what he is going to do. In *Last Tales,* her third volume, Isak Dinesen shifts the doubt to the reader and attempts to ease his burden by guiding his understanding. It is in this collection that we find stories that contain her most explicit statements about art along with stories that deliberately demonstrate artistic principles. Her final volume, *Anecdotes of Destiny,* contains stories that include almost no purely critical commentary and which do not contribute significantly to the illustration of points she has made previously. The reader who has followed Isak Dinesen up to this point will know from the title of the book what he is to expect, and the tales will not disappoint that expectation. They conform to a fully realized aesthetic, an aesthetic that I hope this study may illuminate.

It may seem to readers of Isak Dinesen's works—even to readers of this examination of her aesthetics—that she is, after all, merely moralizing and that she conceives of art merely as the expression of some traditional religious doctrine. This is a misconception that needs to be corrected before any honest consideration of her pronouncements about art can take place. It would be closer to the truth to say that she is offering art as a substitute, rather than as an apology, for religion. No one has been able to assign her beliefs to any single known religion. All that can safely be said is that she believed in a creative force which, for the sake of convenience, she called God.

Aage Henriksen says that if one were to ask her: "When you say God, is it then just a figure of speech or the term for a real universal ruler, then I don't think that she either would or could answer."[3] Her philosophy of life, he says, "exists not as a theory or a system, but only as a shadow of her stories."[4] The cast of this shadow, however, does betray, I think, an un-

---

3. *Guder og galgefugle* (Oslo, 1956), pp. 16–17.
4. Ibid., p. 16.

mistakable religious feeling behind her stories, a feeling which carries over into her critical thinking. It is a pervasive, albeit vague, religiosity that bears, however, no doctrinal stamp.

Because they are more familiar to her, Isak Dinesen draws frequently upon Hebrew and Christian sources for literary metaphor. However, she also acknowledges the influence of Islamic thought, especially in its emphasis on submission, an obligation which figures centrally in her concept of the artist as well as in her philosophy of life. In *Shadows on the Grass,* sequel to the autobiographical *Out of Africa,* she writes:

> In speaking about Mohammedans and Mohammedanism, I am well aware that I got to know in Africa only a primitive, unsophisticated Mohammedanism. Of Mohammedan philosophy or theology I know nothing; from my own experience I can but tell how Islam manifests itself in the course of thought and conduct of the unlearned Orthodox. All the same I feel that you cannot live for a long time among Mohammedans without your own view of life being in some way influenced by theirs.
>
> I have been told that the word "Islam" in itself means submission: the Creed may be defined as the religion which ordains acceptance. And the Prophet does not accept with reluctance or with regret but with rapture. There is in his preaching, as I know it from his unlearned disciples, a tremendous erotic element. . . .
>
> In contrast to many modern Christian ideologies, Islam does not occupy itself with justifying the ways of God to man; its Yes is universal and unconditional. For the lover does not measure the worth of his mistress by a moral or social rod. But the mistress, by absorbing into her own being the dark and dangerous phenomena of life, mysteriously transluminates and sanctifies them, and imbues them with sweetness. . . .
>
> I imagined that just as the erotic aloofness of the founder of Christianity has left his disciples in a kind of void, or of chronic uneasiness and remorse, within this province of life, so has the formidable, indomitable potency of the Prophet pervaded his followers and made mighty latent forces in them fetch headway.[5]

These passages are interesting, I think, in that they are indicative of Isak Dinesen's whole approach to religion. It will be noted that she never went to any particular trouble to find

5. Pp. 28–30.

out about the philosophy or theology of Mohammedanism. What interests her is an attitude which she finds compatible with what life and art have taught her. Similarly, although she had a traditional Lutheran upbringing, her attitude toward Christianity is casual in the sense that she takes from it (and from Judaism) whatever she finds useful. In other words, she does not make art justify religion but religion justify art. This idea is central to Isak Dinesen's thinking; it is what accounts for the constant offense she gave her Catholic secretary Clara Svendsen and it explains those heretical inversions of doctrine that shock the reader of her tales into sudden awareness.

I have thought it wise to arrange the aesthetic theory which I have organized from Isak Dinesen's works according to the process of artistic creation—beginning with the inspiration of the idea, continuing with the expression of the idea in an art form, and concluding with the reception of the idea by the audience. This decision was influenced by the fact that while Isak Dinesen is deeply concerned with the problem of the audience and its proper attitude toward art, her approach to the problem begins with an assessment, first of the artist, and then of art itself.

2

THE INTELLECTUAL DANCE

THE KEY TO Isak Dinesen's aesthetics is to be found, I think, in the relationship between the metaphors of the "bow" and the "blank page" and in the terms *Logos* and *Mythos*. Cardinal Salviati in "The Cardinal's First Tale" (LT) calls the artist "the bow of the Lord"; and the storyteller in "The Blank Page" (LT) says that silence (or the blank page) "tells a finer tale than any of us." In "Converse at Night in Copenhagen" (LT), the poet Johannes Ewald explains to King Christian VII his understanding of the terms *Logos* and *Mythos* as referring respectively to the origin and the manifestation of the artistic impulse. In the interpretation that follows, I hope to demonstrate that Isak Dinesen sees the artist as one who, in surrendering himself to God's will, becomes an implement (bow) in God's hand whereby the divine origin of art (Logos) is manifested in the work of art (Mythos) which will leave in the mind of the audience an impression (blank page) that will reflect the divine origin of the art.

Although I have endeavored to preserve the distinctions between artist, art, and object, it is clear in this case, I think, that a discussion of one is unintelligible without a consideration of the other two. Isak Dinesen is constantly relegating the artist to an inferior position by referring to him in such terms as *servant* and *implement*; and in an effort to know whom he serves and whose instrument he is, it is necessary to know not only "how" he serves but also "what" he serves and to whom he serves it. In the sense that the artist is a "go-between," it can be said that, as Isak Dinesen conceives of him, he goes between God and man—or, more accurately, between Logos, the divine source of his creativity, and the blank page, the residual effect that the audience infers. It is God whom he serves by translating God's Logos into art. This art (or Mythos) is then served to the audience, who will derive from it—but not necessarily see in it—a sense of the divine impulse behind it. Accordingly, it is the purpose of the artist to make the blank page, or ultimate, inferred effect, approximate as nearly as possible the Logos by allowing God to work through him in the creation of his art. It is in this sense that artist, art, and audience are inseparable, just as there can be no music until the bow strokes the string.

The artist, says Cardinal Salviati, is "the bow of the Lord . . . that frail implement, mute in itself, which in the hand of the master will bring out all music that stringed instruments contain, and be at the same time medium and creator." According to this complex metaphor, the artist is inert until activated by divine forces. Once these divine forces move him, he joins with them in the creation of art. The image of the player doubling as instrument is intentional. In the sense that he absorbs from God the creative impulse, he is master; but he is also God's medium. God and the artist share the role of creator, but the artist alone is the medium of creation; and the stringed instrument on which he both plays and is played is the means whereby Logos becomes Mythos.

The artist is mute until "played," but then, too, so is the stringed instrument. Not until the latter is played upon does it send forth all the music that it contains. And even this music is inferior to the idea that produced it. "Previous to speech, and higher than speech," says the poet in "Converse at Night in Copenhagen," "we acknowledge another idea: *logos. Logos,* in Greek, means *Word,* and by the Word all things were created." What emanates from Logos, then, is not the same as Logos but an approximation of it—an imitation of it—what Isak Dinesen means, apparently, by the term *Mythos*. Mythos, in the metaphor of the bow, would be the actual sound of the music.

"Mythos," says the poet, "is the earthly reflection of my heavenly existence. *Mythos*, in Greek, means speech, or, since I was never good at Greek . . . and since scholars may consider me mistaken—you and I, at any rate, for tonight will agree to take it in such a sense." Mythos, as the earthly reflection of heavenly existence, is synonymous with art and can be applied to any visible or audible manifestation of the Logos by which, as the poet says, *all* things were created.

But it is not enough that the artist should be the means whereby the Logos becomes Mythos. The poet in the story sees this function of the artist as only a partial fulfillment of a commandment of God. Beyond this is the equally important consideration of the effect of the artist's Mythos on others. He expresses this idea to the king in the following passage:

"Verily, verily," he cried, "all my life I have loved the Word. Few men have loved it as deeply as I. Its innermost secrets are laid open to me. Therefore, also, a knowledge has been communicated to me. At the moment when my Almighty Father first created me by His word, He demanded and expected from me that I should one day return to Him and bring Him back His word, as speech. That is the one task allotted to me, to fulfill during my time and my course on earth. From his divine Logos— the creative force, the beginning—I shall work out my human mythos—the abiding substance, remembrance. And in time to come, when by His infinite grace I shall once more have become one with Him, then will we look down together from heaven— I myself with tears, but my God with a smile—demanding and expecting that this mythos of mine shall remain after me on earth."

I infer from his passage that the working out of the Mythos serves a double purpose. It reveals to the artist the quality of his own grasp of the Logos, and it transmits to others a reflection (or remembrance) of the Logos which has somehow or other become obscured. If this is what Isak Dinesen is saying (and I think it is), then this elevates art to the level of religion—or even suggests that art is a substitute for religion as a means to God.

It is this means that is symbolized by the blank page. "Where does one read a deeper tale than upon the most perfectly printed page of the most precious book?" asks the storyteller in "The Blank Page." "Upon the blank page." The "deeper tale" of the blank page sounds very much like the poet's description of Logos as "previous to speech, and higher than speech." The difference between the blank page and Logos seems to be one only of position in the process of art from impulse to effect—with Logos as the impulse and the blank page as the effect. Although the complex concept of the blank page must await fuller analysis later, it may be helpful to think of it here as the inferences which the reflecting mind draws from the work of art as it contemplates the total pattern of suggestiveness left unresolved within the work of art itself. By deliberate ambiguity, the artist thus avoids direct statement which, as I see it, Isak Dinesen would not think possible anyway.

"When a royal and gallant pen [the bow]," says the storyteller, "in the moment of its highest inspiration [in the hands of the Lord], has written down its tale [Mythos] with the rarest ink of all—where, then, may one read a still deeper, sweeter, merrier and more cruel tale [Logos] than that? Upon the blank page." The blank is, in effect, the uniting with God of what Robert Langbaum calls the "intellectual dance of Logos and speech."[1]

There is a contradiction, and I think a deliberate one, between what Isak Dinesen says about the artist in her tales and the effect she strives to achieve through her tales. Hannah Arendt believes that Isak Dinesen learned from her own life to avoid being imprisoned in one identity, and that she carried this over into her art by purposely obscuring her identity as

---

1. *The Gayety of Vision* (New York, 1965), p. 244.

author of the tales and as storyteller in the tales.[2] Miss Arendt implies that the reason for this is a desire to emphasize effect. However, within the tales themselves Isak Dinesen is intensely concerned with the artist, even though the ultimate obligation of the artist is to disappear from the scene, to return to the state of the "mute implement" and let silence speak.

This contradiction between a preoccupation with the artist within many of the tales and an emphasis on effect as the purpose of the tale can be resolved, I think, if we make a distinction between the artist as subject matter and the artist as intruder. Isak Dinesen is concerned about the artist who "gives himself away,"[3] and she is eager to warn him against making his presence felt in the work he is creating. The effect of the eloquent blank page will not be achieved if the artist intrudes himself into the work, draws attention to himself, or in any way interferes with his function as the "bow of the Lord." When the bow is drawn across the strings, it is not the bow that is to be noticed, nor even the strings; it is the music—and beyond that, the effect of the music which is something other than the music itself. Isak Dinesen, therefore, is concerned that the artist remember his modesty and allow nothing to hinder the communication between the Logos and the blank page.

To retain such modesty he must remain loyal to the Logos, or story, as I think Isak Dinesen defines it. " 'Be loyal to the story,' " says the old hag in "The Blank Page" to her storyteller daughter. " 'Be eternally and unswervingly loyal to the story . . . Where the storyteller is loyal, eternally and unswervingly loyal to the story, there, in the end, silence will speak. Where the story has been betrayed, silence is but

---

2. "Isak Dinesen: 1885-1962," *New Yorker* (9 November 1968), p. 223.

3. *Karen Blixen Fortaeller* (phonograph record), Louisiana/Gyldendal Grammofonplader. Isak Dinesen used this phrase in reference to an appearance on American television. She felt that such exposure could violate the delicate art of the storyteller by focusing attention upon him rather than upon the story.

emptiness. But we, the faithful, when we have spoken our last word, will hear the voice of silence.' "

Beyond this artistic principle there is a philosophical one too, which helps to explain why Isak Dinesen pays so much attention to the role of the artist. When the poet Johannes Ewald talks of working out his human Mythos from the divine Logos and bringing God's word back to him, he is implying in the term *"human" Mythos* a meaning that includes more than artistic creation. He is implying a mode of behavior, an "art" of life. And in the play *The Revenge of Truth,* which is performed in "The Roads Round Pisa" (SGT), the witch Amiane talks about "all of us" and the importance of our "keeping the ideas of the author clear. . . . This," she says, "is the real happiness of life." The philosophical implication is, of course that all of us are potential artists with the ability to keep the ideas of the author (God) clear. However, since most of us never realize this potential, it falls, apparently, to those who do (the artists) to remind us through art and by means of the blank page what those ideas are.

What all of this means here, I think, is that Isak Dinesen's primary concern is in setting forth the obligations, rewards, and restraints of the artist as she deduces them from her concept of him as a "mute implement in the hands of the Lord," the liaison between God and man (or Logos and blank page), and, as she calls him in "The Deluge at Norderney" (SGT), "the arbiter on reality."

II

THE BOW OF THE LORD

3

MASQUERADE AND REALITY

IN A LITTLE play, *Sandhedens Haevn (The Revenge of Truth),* written long before she was to achieve fame with her first collection of tales, Isak Dinesen expresses an idea that most critics have interpreted as the governing principle behind her attitude toward life and art. Early in the play, the witch Amiane comes forth to state this idea in a speech which is also included in "The Roads Round Pisa" (SGT) as the central motif of that story.

"The truth, my children, is that we are, all of us, acting in a marionette comedy. What is important more than anything else in a marionette comedy, is keeping the ideas of the author clear. This is the real happiness of life, and now that I have at last come into a marionette play, I will never go out of it again. But you, my fellow actors, keep the ideas of the author clear. Aye, drive them to their utmost consequences."

Such critics as Aage Henriksen, Erik Johannesson, and Robert Langbaum have explored the ramifications of this statement and have argued convincingly against the over-simplified interpretation of the statement as advocating either determinism or blind acceptance.[1] I mention it here, not to

1. Aage Henriksen, "Karen Blixen og Marionetterne," in *Det Guddommelige Barn og Andre Essays om Karen Blixen* (Copenhagen, 1965),

19

add unnecessarily to that discussion, but because I think it is of
some importance to understand that Isak Dinesen does believe
that man has a primary possibility in life which it is his duty
to discover and to exploit. He is equally free not to discover
this possibility and not to exploit it, but his greatest happiness
comes from believing that there is an author and a play and
that the role he is to assume is the only possible one for him.

The author to whom the witch refers is specifically the
human author of the marionette comedy, but it is obvious,
I think, that she is also referring to God as the author of life.
The fusion of the two meanings in the single word is the beginning of Isak Dinesen's critical thinking, for stemming from
this comparison between God and the artist are all the
principles by which she judges art. Although both God and
the artist are authors, the artist is not master of the situation,
for he has, says Johannes Rosendahl, "an adversary in a
greater artist—in God."[2] The artist is, himself, a character in
God's greater story, and as such he is as much obliged as
anyone else to "keep the ideas of the author clear. For Isak
Dinesen, God is the greatest artist."[3] "It is He who will finally
read the last proof."[4] As Rosendahl puts it: "God is the poet,
the artist in whom man must put himself."[5]

It is not surprising, then, that Isak Dinesen should see
the offices of priest and poet as reverse sides of the same coin.
In "The Cardinal's First Tale" (LT), she affirms the insepar-
ableness of the two offices in the character of Cardinal Salviati,
whose personality contains a strong mixture of both. When the
lady in black asks him, "Who are you?", he must tell her a
strange story, in the midst of which he asks: "Who, Madame,
is the man who is placed, in his life on earth, with his back

pp. 9–32. Erik Johannesson, in *The World of Isak Dinesen* (Seattle,
1961), pp. 81–89. Robert Langbaum, in *The Gayety of Vision* (New
York, 1965), pp. 38–72.

2. *Karen Blixen: Fire Foredrag* (Copenhagen, 1957), p. 46.

3. Jorgen Gustava Brandt, "Et Essay om Karen Blixen," *Heretica,* VI
(1953), no. 2, p. 201.

4. Rosendahl, p. 46.

5. Ibid., p. 47.

to God and his face to man, because he is God's mouthpiece, and through him the voice of God is given forth? Who is the man who has no existence of his own—because the existence of each human being is his—and who has neither home nor friends nor wife—because his hearth is the hearth of and he himself is the friend and lover of all human beings?" The lady's reply to this question is "the artist," to which the cardinal adds that it is also the priest.

The cardinal is well qualified to talk about the poet-priest relationship because he has been trained to be both. He and his twin brother were intended at birth to be, one an artist and the other a priest. But the death of one brother in a fire and the resulting confusion of identities has led to the other's being educated officially for the priesthood but unofficially for the role of artist. Through this man Isak Dinesen is able to express not only the Apollonian-Dionysian tension in both artist and priest but also to reveal how both share, along with the aristocrat, a separation from ordinary society as well as an obligation to a destiny that differs significantly from that of the rest of mankind. In fulfilling their own destinies, these are the only persons who consciously lead others to fulfill theirs. In a world where all destinies were obvious, the artist, the priest, and the aristocrat would have no reason to exist.

Because his back is to God and he serves as God's mouthpiece, the artist, as well as the priest and the aristocrat, must share something of God's loneliness and risk; and he is denied certain advantages that other men are free to enjoy, among these the possibility of remorse and the possession of honor. "Certain spiritual benefits granted to other human beings, are indeed withheld," says the cardinal, but he also reminds the lady in black that the Lord indemnifies his mouthpiece. "If he is without potency, he has been given a small bit of omnipotence." And he adds:

"Calmly, like a child in his father's house binding and loosening his favorite dogs, he will bind the influence of Pleiades and loose the bands of Orion. Like a child in his father's house ordering about his servants, he will send lightnings, that they may go and say to him: 'Here we are.' Just as the gate of the citadel is opened to the vice-regent, the gates of death have been opened to him. And as the heir apparent will have been entrusted with the regalia of the King, he knows where light dwells, and as to darkness, where is the place thereof."

It is in such stories as "Sorrow-Acre" (WT) and "Converse at Night in Copenhagen" (LT) that Isak Dinesen includes the aristocrat in her category of God's mouthpieces. Of all people in Copenhagen," says the poet Johannes Ewald in "Converse," "very likely you and I, the monarch and the poet, are the two who come nearest to being almighty." Lonely and slightly mad, young King Christian VII, whom Ewald is addressing, is the poet's perfect counterpart. In their vastly different ways both men bear a burden of responsibility to man and God that is not shared by either man or God. The inclusion of the aristocrat in the triumvirate of those who stand in lieu of God is important because it points up the fact that even those who rule in God's place are not free from the exigencies of mortality. The old lord in "Sorrow-Acre" (WT) explains patiently to his impatient nephew Adam that although the aristocrat bears the same responsibility to those beneath him as the gods do to those beneath them, the aristocrat is still subject, like all men, to the will of the gods.

Isak Dinesen makes the sharpest distinction between the functions of God and the artist when, in "The Deluge at Norderney" (SGT), the valet disguised as a cardinal refers to God as the arbiter of the masquerade and to the artist as the arbiter on reality. As arbiter of the masquerade, God has a taste for disguises and prefers his creatures to respect his mask and their own rather than attempt to give back to him the truth which he knows already. To reveal the truth is his prerogative, and the day on which he chooses to reveal the truth will be the day of judgment—"the hour in which the Almighty God himself lets fall the mask," as the disguised valet puts it. The masks behind which God conceals the truth are everywhere present in nature, but they are not always readily apparent to man. The person best equipped, it seems, to perceive the masks that pervade reality is the artist; and it is his function, as the arbiter on reality, to make these masks apparent as masks, in a way that leads not to any explicable truth behind the masks, but rather to an acceptance of the presence behind the masks of a truth which we are not privileged to understand. Thus, mask stands between truth and reality, and the art that makes these masks apparent is a higher reality because it is closer to truth.

The process of discovering the masks within reality seems to me to be somewhat like the children's game in which one is asked to study a drawing and find as many faces as he can in what looks at first glance to be merely a landscape. It is the artist who is most adept at discerning these faces, or masks, and when he points them out to us to our satisfaction, we find that we can no longer look at the landscape without seeing the faces. After a while it may even be difficult for us to see the landscape at all or believe that we ever could have seen it and nothing else. The faces then become more important than the landscape; the landscape exists only to contain the faces; and although we know no more about the truth behind the drawing than we did before, we cannot deny the presence of the faces nor the effect they give to the drawing, which is to make it seem whole and proper only when they are in it. God, as arbiter of the masquerade, draws the faces and then obscures them in the landscape—they are, in effect, His masks—and the artist, as arbiter on reality, fills in the drawing in such a way that the landscape reveals the masks.

Part of the risk inherent to this distinction is, I think, that of failure on the part of the artist to perceive the mask or, perceiving it, not to re-create it authentically. Or he may go the other way and see more faces than are really there, thus misrepresenting God with false images. A much greater risk, however, stems from the artist's disadvantage of not knowing any more of the truth behind the mask than any other man. As Johannes Rosendahl says: "The decisive factor is: Will

they [the artists] tell their own story or God's?"[6] The artist
is not "master of the situation"[7] as God is; thus he must work
without the assurance that God has, that he is doing the right
thing.

The weight of the risk is heavy, and in a character such
as Charlie Despard, who appears in both "The Young Man
with a Carnation" (WT) and "A Consolatory Tale" (WT),
Isak Dinesen portrays the artist in the throes of wrestling with
his responsibility and in danger of lapsing into despair. "I have
had to read the Book of Job, to get strength to bear my responsibility at all," says Despard to Aeneas Snell in "A Consolatory
Tale." "Do you see yourself in the place of Job, Charlie?"
asks Aeneas. "No," says Despard solemnly and proudly, "in
the place of the Lord."

Hans Brix in *Blixens Eventyr* [8] feels that Isak Dinesen
identified very closely with the character of Charlie Despard.
His very initials suggest her own (Karen Christentze Dinesen),
and his situation in "The Young Man with the Carnation,"
the story that introduces her second volume of stories, *Winter's
Tales,* resembles her own just prior to its publication. He is
a writer whose first book was a success and who is now worried about his second. "A Consolatory Tale," which concludes
Winter's Tales, shows a still questioning but more confident
Despard fusing his ideas with those of the equally adept storyteller, Aeneas Snell. Their ideas about storytelling, although
different, are really merely two ways of arriving at the same
end.

By identifying the artist with the Lord in the story of
Job, Isak Dinesen further isolates him from the society of
ordinary men and establishes him as a person of extraordinary
obligations. Developing his analogy, Despard explains his
theory to Aeneas Snell. "I have behaved to my reader as the
Lord behaves to Job," he says. "I have laid a wager with Satan
about the soul of my reader. I have marred his path and turned

---

6. *Karen Blixen: Fire Foredrag,* p. 46.

7. Ibid.

8. (Copenhagen, 1949), p. 159.

terrors upon him, caused him to ride on the wind and dissolved his substance, and when he waited for light there was darkness."

What Despard does not say, but what we, as readers, remember, is that the artist as man is not spared Job's lot. There is, therefore, a double burden upon him. While he may hold with the valet Kasparson, who is disguised as a cardinal in "The Deluge at Norderney," that the mask of God will fall away on the day of judgment and the voice in the whirlwind take on meaning, he knows, furthermore, that the answer to the mysteries which his art presents are also locked in that voice and behind that mask. It is the artist's task, apparently, to convey an awareness of the mysteries, but it is not in his power either to know or to dispense secrets.

When the lady in black in "The Cardinal's First Tale" sighs at the lot of the artist, the cardinal tells her not to have pity on him.

"The servant was neither forced nor lured into service. Before taking him on, his Master spoke straightly and fairly to him. 'You are aware,' he said, 'that I am almighty. And you have before you the world which I have created. Now give me your opinion on it. Do you take it that I have meant to create a peaceful world?' 'No, my Lord,' the candidate replied. 'Or that I have,' the Lord asked, 'meant to create a pretty and neat world?' 'No, indeed,' answered the youth. 'Or a world easy to live in?' asked the Lord. 'O good Lord, no!' said the candidate. 'Or do you,' the Lord asked for the last time, 'hold and believe that I have resolved to create a sublime world, with all things necessary to the purpose in it, and none left out?' 'I do,' said the young man. 'Then,' said the Master, 'then, my servant and mouthpiece, take the oath!' "

A similar dialogue with the Lord in "The Young Man with the Carnation" brings Despard to the point where he is ready to accept the Lord's covenant. Again the Lord's preliminary questioning is rendered by Isak Dinesen in the manner of God's dialogue with Job.

"Who made the ships, Charlie?" he asked. "Nay, I know not," said Charlie, "did you make them?" "Yes," said the Lord, "I made the ships on their keels, and all floating things. The moon that sails in the sky, the orbs that swing in the universe, the tides, the generations, the fashions. You make me laugh, for I have given you all the world to sail and float in, and you have run aground here, in a room of the Queen's Hotel to seek a quarrel."

It is at this point that the Lord makes it clear to Despard that the artist creates not for himself or his public but for God because, as Peter says in "Peter and Rosa" (WT): "If the work of God does not glorify him, how can God be glorious?" Aage Henriksen says that this question is an assertion and that the assertion immediately has consequences for the poet who, in his works, has put himself in the place of God. The storyteller, says Henriksen, is Providence for the persons that he tells about and can see to it that they get what they deserve. However, Henriksen asks, "What does man deserve, and what can he in reality get? An explanation? Justice? Grace?"[9] These questions, Henriksen goes on to say, cannot be answered except by what he calls "artistic evidence."[10]

Artistic evidence is much like the Lord's answer to Charlie Despard. It is not an answer at all, really, but an injunction not to expect answers; and before it Despard is silenced. With the discussion thus ended, Despard is ready to enter into a pact with the Lord in which the Lord makes it clear that the purpose of art is not to explain Him but to glorify Him.

"Come," said the Lord again, "I will make a covenant between me and you. I, I will not measure you out any more distress than you need to write your books." "Oh, indeed!" said Charlie. "What did you say?" asked the Lord. "Do you want any less than that?" "I said nothing," said Charlie. "But you are to write the books," said the Lord. "For it is I who want them written. Not the public, not by any means the critics, but ME!" "Can I be certain of that?" Charlie asked. "Not always," said the Lord. "You will not be certain of it at all times. But I tell you now that it is so. You will have to hold on to that." "O good God," said Charlie. "Are you going," said the Lord, "to thank me for what I have done for

9. *Guder og galgefugle* (Oslo, 1956), p. 16.
10. Ibid.

you tonight?" "I think," said Charlie, "that we will leave it at what it is, and say no more about it."

In addition to the Lord's insistence that Despard write for Him, there are two important points in this last dialogue that are fundamental to Isak Dinesen's concept of the artist. One has to do with the "measure of distress" that the Lord promises to dispense in quantities just sufficient to result in the production of art (and which is discussed at length in Part II, chapter 5). The other is Despard's reluctance to thank the Lord for what the Lord has agreed to do. This last point is pertinent here in clarification of the relationship between God and artist. In not allowing Despard to show gratitude to God, Isak Dinesen is, in effect, denying the artist the comfort of common piety. What she implies is that the distresses measured out to the artist balance any rewards. One does not show gratitude, she seems to say, for a dearly purchased gift.

Besides bestowing the gift of creativity on the artist, God also supplies him with the raw material out of which he can create fictional characters that can outlive God's own mortal ones. In a story within the story "The Roads Round Pisa," the librettist Monti is replying to a Monsignor Talbot who has just asked Monti if he really does believe himself to be a creator in the same sense as God.

"God!" Monti cried, "God! Do you not know that what God really wants to create in my Don Giovanni, and the Odysseus of Homer, and Cervantes's knight? Very likely those are the only people for whom heaven and hell have ever been made, for you cannot imagine that an Almighty God would go on forever and ever, world without end, with my mother-in-law and the Emperor of Austria? Humanity, the men and women of this earth, are only the plaster of God, and we, the artists, are his tools, and when the statue is finished in marble or bronze, he breaks us all up. When you die you will probably go out like a candle, with nothing left, but in the mansions of eternity will walk Orlando, the Misanthrope and my Donna Elvira. Such is God's plan of work, and if we find it somehow slow, who are we that we should criticize him, seeing that we know nothing whatever of time or eternity?"

In creating such imaginative and enduring characters,

the artist is, however, not exceeding God's imagination but rather entering into it. Erik Johannesson says that in Isak Dinesen's world "God is the greatest artist because he has the greatest imagination. . . . When her characters . . . recognize their limitations and affirm the power of God, they affirm the artist and the story, for God is the greatest storyteller of them all."[11]

When an artist is at his best, he is exhibiting what the valet disguised as a cardinal in "The Deluge at Norderney" calls the "tremendous courage of the Creator of this world." The artist is closest to God and to the creative spirit when he is exercising, in the words of Adam in "Sorrow-Acre," "Imagination, daring, and passion." "Your stories are over our stories," says Charlie Despard; and this acknowledgement leads Johannes Rosendahl to note the obligation on the part of the artist to rise above the triviality of life and its banal claims and to concentrate on the "story."[12]

God's envy of man's creation as expressed by Monti in "The Roads Round Pisa" is balanced by what the valet/cardinal in "The Deluge at Norderney" goes on to say about man's envy of God.

"Every human being has, I believe, at times given room to the idea of creating a world himself. The Pope, in a flattering way, encouraged these thoughts in me when I was a young man. I reflected then that I might, had I been given omnipotence and a free hand, have made a fine world. I might have bethought me of the trees and rivers, of the different keys in music, of friendship, and innocence; but upon my word and honor, I should not have dared to arrange these matters of love and marriage as they are, and my world should have lost sadly thereby. What an overwhelming lesson to all artists! Be not afraid of absurdity; do not shrink from the fantastic. Within a dilemma, choose the most unheard-of, the most dangerous, solution. Be brave, be brave! Ah, Madame, we have got much to learn."

The idea of creating a world himself occurred also, we

---

11. *The World of Isak Dinesen* (Seattle, 1961), p. 125.
12. *Karen Blixen: Fire Foredrag*, p. 46. ("Men 'Historien,' ikke Livets Trivialitet og banale Opretholdelse, er disse Menneskers Sigte.")

know, to Satan who did not shrink from absurdity or the fantastic. In Isak Dinesen's concept of the artist there is a trace of the diabolical, and Louis E. Grandjean points out in *Blixens Animus* that she shared with Nietzsche the belief that the satanic are preferable to the good who do not create, since the diabolical create more than they destroy.[13] Even Cardinal Salviati in "The Cardinal's First Tale" must confess to the lady in black that he is not sure it is God he serves.

It is probably the painter Cazotte in "Ehrengard" who best illustrates the presence of the diabolical in the artist. While in the midst of a scheme to humiliate Ehrengard, he betrays his peculiarly mixed loyalties in a letter to the Countess von Gassner.

P.S. Walking in the garden this evening Prince Lothar said to Princess Ludmilla: "So here is Paradise." And with her head upon his shoulder his young wife echoed: "Paradise." I smiled benevolence on them, like an archangel assisting the Lord in laying out the garden of Eden, and smiling on the first human male and female. But the great landscape architect himself, when his work had been completed, on looking at it and listening to the Gloria and Hallelujah of his angelic chorus, will have felt the craving for a clear, unbiased eye to view it with him, the eye of a critic, a connoisseur and an arbiter. With what creature, in all Paradise, will he have found that eye, Madame? Madame—with the Serpent!

If the Serpent had been content to be nothing more than critic, connoisseur, and arbiter, he would very much have resembled the artist who, as the old artist in "Copenhagen Season" (LT) tells his drawing-room audience, would not have been shocked by the nakedness of Adam and Eve. But there is a vital difference between the two. The artist turns his passive observations into action by re-creating what he sees; the Serpent steps out of his role as passive observer into the role of active manipulator by interfering in what he sees.

Thus, Cazotte might resemble an archangel when he is busily arranging the Eden-like retreat at Rosenbad, and he is

13. (Copenhagen, 1957), p. 53.

the balanced artist when he is painting scenes and portraits; but the diabolical begins to overpower him at the time he is painting Ehrengard's portrait without her knowledge and for impure reasons; and it consumes him completely once his plan to seduce Ehrengard—albeit symbolically— is put into practice. In so doing, however, Cazotte leaves himself vulnerable to the prophecy in the Garden which foretells that the woman shall conquer. His plan fails, and the victory goes to Ehrengard.

To say that Cazotte has confused life with art, has tried to mix the two, has endeavored to alchemize art into life is to say that he has tried to usurp God's role as arbiter of the masquerade. Life, Isak Dinesen insists, is God's story, and he will dress it as he sees fit and with greater imagination. Any attempt to invade his domain will result in surprise and failure for the interloper. Out of the raw material of His imagination God has fashioned creation and given it to man as the raw material out of which man, as artist, may fashion art. As God respects the artist by refusing to turn reality into art, so must the artist respect God by resisting the temptation to turn art into reality.

The efficacy of this mandate is the express concern not only of "Ehrengard" but also of "The Immortal Story" (AD) and "The Poet" (SGT). "The Immortal Story" is the tale of an old man, Mr. Clay, who deliberately sets about turning a traditional sailor's yarn into reality. For years sailors have told each other about how, during shore leave, they were picked up by an elderly man, carried to his lavish home, plied with the finest food and wines, and then given five pounds to sleep with the old man's lovely young wife. When Mr. Clay is told this story by his faithful clerk, Elishama, and it is explained to him that the story has no truth in it, Mr. Clay will not rest until he sees the story enacted before his eyes with himself in the role of the impotent old man.

With the able assistance of his clerk, Mr. Clay manages, not without some difficulty, to hire the services of a prostitute and to pick up a young sailor from the waterfront. The fact that old Mr. Clay must hire a prostitute because he does not have a wife is only the first of many ways in which the story changes as it is brought to life. Two attempts to pick up a sailor fail, and when they finally do find one who will cooperate, it is one who is more interested in the money than in the adventure. The sailor is on the point of leaving several times during dinner, but he is persuaded to stay only to surprise everyone by falling in love with the prostitute. The following morning he finds it difficult to see any resemblance between what has happened to him and the story he has heard (and told) many times at sea. But once he does see the connection, he insists that he will never tell what happened to him because surely no one would ever believe it.

The yarn as it has always been told is a mask made visible by the storyteller through his arbitrary use of reality. But once that mask is violated, is forced to become real, it vanishes and a different mask takes its place. The new story is a totally different story. It is not the story of a sailor's dream but of an old man's desire to impose his will upon life. Ironically, the old man dies during the night, and his death reveals that a greater imagination than his is directing the story.

As an imaginary arrangement of incidents and characters to conform to the ideas of the storyteller, the story is safe. But the moment the story takes life, the moment the imagination of the artist comes in conflict with the imagination of God, the artist loses control over it and usually suffers in the bargain. I think the evidence is clear that Isak Dinesen would scorn those who would take her views on aristocracy and acceptance too personally and try to pattern their lives in accordance with those of any of her characters. The artist's job, as she sees it, is not to show man how to live but to heighten his consciousness of the life he is already living.

Councilor Mathiesen in "The Poet" (SGT) repeats Cazotte's and Mr. Clay's mistake but with direr consequences. To compensate for his own failure as a poet, Mathiesen meddles in the life of the genuine young poet, Anders Kube. He hopes by interfering to guide Kube towards higher poetic

powers and thereby experience vicariously the fruits of success. In order to accomplish this end, Mathiesen decides to
marry the young widow Fransine because he knows that she
and Kube have fallen in love, and he feels that such a melancholy romantic situation will stimulate Kube to new lyrical
heights. As his plan takes shape, however, a greater imagination than his assumes control and brings about a quite different story. Mathiesen does not know that Kube plans to commit
suicide on the day of the wedding. Nor does he anticipate that
his scheme to have Fransine disrobe before her lover on the
night before the wedding will result in disaster and death.

The idea for the midnight disrobing is an idea which
Mathiesen has taken from a popular and highly controversial
German romantic novel of the day.[14] By so doing, Mathiesen
is giving another turn of the screw to the theme of life imi-
tating art. Life, of course, departs radically from art when
Kube spurns Fransine and then uses the suicide gun to shoot
the voyeur Mathiesen. Bleeding profusely, the councilor crawls
back to the house to which Fransine has fled and tries to con-
vince her with his dying breath that the world is still beautiful
and good. Because it suits him that the world should be lovely,
he means to conjure it into being so. But Fransine knows that
the world of which he speaks is really the world in which
Anders Kube will be hanged for murder, and in her anguish
she lifts up a large stone and crushes Mathiesen's head. "You,"
she cries at him. "You Poet!"

The epithet is bitterly ironic because Mathiesen is the
antithesis of Isak Dinesen's true artist. He has usurped God's
role by taking Kube into his own hands, and he has violated
the mask by forcing reality upon it. Mathiesen dies with his

---

14. *Wally: Die Zweiflerin (Wally: The Doubting Girl)* by Karl Gutzkow
(Mannheim, 1835). Now available in a facsimile edition (Göttingen,
1965). This novel, written partly in diary form, raised a storm of pro-
test because of its heroine's outspoken views on religion and sex. Wally
confesses atheism and advocates free love. The disrobing scene and its
bloody aftermath in "The Poet" parallel closely similar scenes in *Wally*,
which in turn, reflect similar incidents in *Parzifal*. The style of Gutzkow's novel would appeal to one of Isak Dinesen's temperament. She
obviously borrowed the theme and then gave it her own unique twist.

hand outstretched to touch Fransine's heel while she stands above him, the conquering woman. The scene is Isak Dinesen's most graphic illustration of the Biblical prophecy and her own relentless assertion of the evil of exceeding the limits of art. In "Ehrengard" and "The Immortal Story" only the perpetrators suffer, but in "The Poet" the suffering extends to others. In the confusion of mask and reality, the innocent lovers become murderers. The true artist knows that masquerade and reality are antithetical, and he strives to keep them separate by infusing his masquerade with a higher reality that is in direct contrast to the reality of the senses.

4

PRIDE AND HUMILITY

IN A DISCUSSION of Isak Dinesen's tale "The Poet" (SGT), and of the idea reiterated towards the end of it that God is an artist, Johannes Rosendahl says that as an artist God can surely seem incomprehensibly cruel but that suffering is merely a detail in a greater whole. He goes on to explain that, as he interprets Isak Dinesen, man will find peace of mind only by accepting the total work of the great artist. He quotes Councilor Mathiesen, the central figure in the story, who says in the midst of his misery: "And still this was right, in one way or another it was the right arrangement."[1] This total vision, Rosendahl explains, is germane to Isak Dinesen's concept of the artist; and he quotes her as having once said: "Above all people the poet understands this—in the highest pride and the deepest humility—and thus he is made a part of God's nature."[2]

Isak Dinesen is fond of dealing in antithetical terms, and she has made it quite clear, in "A Consolatory Tale" (WT), that she looks upon opposites as locked caskets, each of which contains the key to the other. The dialectic of pride and humil-

1. *Karen Blixen: Fire Foredrag* (Copenhagen, 1957), p. 24.
2. Ibid., p. 24.

THE DIALECTS OF PRIDE AND HUMILITY

it is one of her most profound concepts, for the artist's relationship to these poles determines what he shall do with the part of God's nature which he shares. Pride, as Isak Dinesen sees it, is understanding the work of God as being the "right arrangement"; humility is understanding that within this arrangement God has no favorites. She excludes no man from the possibility of sharing in God's nature; she says simply that the man who is most sensitive to the rightness of things, who is equally proud and humble before such rightness, is the man we call an artist.

Isak Dinesen's best expression of her concept of pride is contained in a passage from *Out of Africa*. John Davenport calls it "quintessential Blixen."

Pride is faith in the idea that God had, when he made us. A proud man is conscious of the idea, and aspires to realize it. He does not strive towards a happiness, or comfort, which may be irrelevant to God's idea of him. His success is the idea of God, successfully carried through, and he is in love with his destiny. As the good citizen finds his happiness in the fulfillment of his duty to the community so does the proud man his happiness in the fulfillment of his fate.

People who have no pride are not aware of any idea of God in the making of them, and sometimes they make you doubt that there has ever been much of an idea, or else it has been lost, and who shall find it again? They have got to accept as success what others warrant to be so, and to take their happiness, and even their own selves, at the quotation of the day. They tremble, with reason, before their fate. (P. 261)

These two paragraphs on pride "not only record an attitude of life," says Donald Hannah, "they are also the expression of an artistic creed."[3] Loyalty to the story, to the ideas of the author, to a greater imagination, are among the familiar ideas in Isak Dinesen that are implicit in this statement.

Also implicit in this statement on pride is the danger of overconfidence, of smugness, of falling into the error of feeling that God has singled you out for a higher purpose, has bestowed special favors on you with their attendant privileges.

---

3. "In Memoriam Karen Blixen," *Sewanee Review,* LXXI no. 4 (Autumn 1963), p. 602.

Throughout her tales, Isak Dinesen repeatedly warns against this fallacy, and she guarded against it in her own life by renouncing faith and hope at times when they would seem to have been the only things left to cling to. Glenway Wescott records her as having once said to Marianne Moore: " 'When you have a great and difficult task, something perhaps almost impossible, if you only work a little at a time, every day a little, *without faith and without hope*'—and she underlined these words with her spooky, strong, but insubstantial voice— 'suddenly the work will finish itself.' "[4]

What she is concerned with in this remark is the danger of a temptation to which the artist is particularly prone—that is, the temptation to believe that the creative talent carries with it its own assurances of success and its own protection from despair. As she sees it, such an attitude can only lead to despair and failure, for it misleads the artist into expecting certain benefits without suffering—or into interpreting his suffering as a promise of forthcoming benefits. In renouncing faith and hope at such moments of temptation, the artist is putting himself in a position to be "inspired."

The idea of receiving the artistic "inspiration" without deliberately seeking it or feeling specially favored, by renouncing faith and hope, is akin to the Christian idea of grace as a state one arrives at through submission to the will of Providence. It is an awakening, a realization rather than a predetermined goal, and it comes about only after the true and total abandonment of ambition. It is "Thy will be done" without any wish to contravene that will, without any real assurance that one's submission is absolute, and without any guarantee of approval. It is in this state that "the work will finish itself."

The artist who considers himself favored is, in effect, presuming that he knows God's plan in advance. It is one thing to believe that there is a plan and that it is right, but quite another to believe one can anticipate that plan; or, sensing at any

---

4. "Isak Dinesen tells a tale," *Harper's Magazine,* CCXX, no. 1318 (March 1960), p. 72.

given moment one's part in that plan, to assume that that part will not change. Such foreknowledge would violate the mystery of existence, and certainly, as Isak Dinesen conceives of it, the function of the artist is not to violate but to vindicate the mystery.

It is his awareness of the fallacy of considering himself favored that prevents Cardinal Salviati in "The Cardinal's First Tale" (LT) from giving the lady in black an unequivocal answer to her question about his identity. He is no more sure, in his role as priest, that he was intended to be a priest than he would have been sure, in the role of artist, that he had been intended to be an artist. A man has many possibilities, but only one destiny, and he must work at the role he has assumed, it seems, without the assurance, without even the hope,[5] that he has assumed correctly. He will then take pride in aspiring to realize the idea God had when He made him, but he will at the same time be humbled by the knowledge that aspiration is not fulfillment. If fulfillment is achieved, then pride and humility are reconciled into happiness.

It is humility that prevents the artist from stepping outside the boundaries of art, which makes him accept the distress and take the risks that attend the creation of art, and which tests his confidence at every turn. "Are you sure," asks the lady in black of Cardinal Salviati, "that it is God whom you serve?" "That," he says, "that, Madame, is a risk which the artists and priests of the world have to run." It is in the risk, it would seem, that artistic honesty is born. The self-appointed artist will lapse into the arrogance of presuming that his art is good simply because he has made it. The God-appointed artist can never be that certain. He will proceed with caution, always sensitive to the forces at work within him, always fearful lest he presume too much. Therefore, he will wait upon the outcome of his art and know its worth by its reception. A poet is

---

5. I think Isak Dinesen would distinguish between hope and submission by defining hope as the desire to fulfill one's own wishes as opposed to submission which is the desire to fulfill God's wishes. Hope, which is directed towards some predetermined satisfaction, cannot coexist with submission, which anticipates nothing.

known by his poetry, in other words, and not by his preten-
sions.

An example of the pretentious, self-appointed poet is
Baron Gersdorff who appears in an inset tale in "The Deluge
at Norderney" (SGT). The baron is the mentor of a boy
named Jonathan Maersk, and his plans for the boy go awry in
the way that all the plans of all meddlers do in Isak Dinesen's
tales. The baron is a man of fashion, and people of fashion,
although they crowd the pages of Isak Dinesen's stories, are
never themselves artists. In their shame, says Jonathan, Adam
and Eve concerned themselves with matters of fashion, and
this concern is a symbol of their involvement in the affairs of
the nonartistic world, for the artist is not shocked by nakedness. " 'You know me . . . to be a poet,' " the baron explains to
a friend. " 'Well, I will tell you what sort of poet I am. I have
never in my life written a line without imagining myself in the
place of some poet or other that I know of.' "

That it is impossible, according to Isak Dinesen, to be a
poet under such circumstances is made clear in the following
passage from "The Poet" (SGT). The speaker, Count Augustus von Schimmelmann, whose youthful poetic leanings
were presented in "The Roads Round Pisa" (SGT), is, in this
story, a middle-aged man who has come to realize that he is
not a poet after all and has profited from his awareness. He is
expressing his views to Councilor Mathiesen who, as we have
already seen, arrives too late at the same awareness.

"I have, as you may know, some time since given up any artistic
ambitions and have been occupying myself, within the sphere of
the arts, with connoisseurship." (He was indeed a shrewd critic
of all objects of art.) "Here I have learned that it is not possible
to paint any definite object, say, a rose, so that I, or any other
intelligent critic, shall not be able to decide, within twenty years,
at what period it was painted, or more or less, at what place on
the earth. The artist has meant to create either a picture of a rose
in the abstract, or the portrait of a particular rose; it is never in
the least his intention to give us a Chinese, Persian, or Dutch,
or, according to the period, a rococo or a pure Empire rose. If I
told him that this was what he had done, he would not understand

me. He might be angry with me. He would say: 'I have painted a rose.' Still he cannot help it. I am thus so far superior to the artist that I can mete him with a measure of which he himself knows nothing. At the same time I could not paint, and hardly see or conceive, a rose myself. I might imitate any of their creations. I might say: 'I will paint a rose in the Chinese or Dutch or in the rococo manner.' But I should never have the courage to paint a rose as it looks. For how does a rose look?"

Among the many interesting things in this passage, two are pertinent to this discussion. One is the fact that, unlike the baron or the councilor, whose lack of talent leads them either to imitate or to manipulate others, Count Augustus has moved to the more realistic position of critic. Aware that he is unable to paint a rose intuitively, that he is lacking in original talent, he refuses to become the self-appointed artist who paints according to a school. He prefers, instead, to be the guardian of originality and the bestower of labels.

The other point of interest, one that is not apparent from this passage alone but which emerges after a comparison of this passage with ones in the earlier story, "The Roads Round Pisa," is that Count Augustus has shifted his concept of the source of the artistic impulse from a belief that the mirror gives the best image of truth to a belief in some process of intuition. Since Count Augustus is described by the author as a person who "took to living, so to say, upon the envy of the outside world, and to accept his happiness according to the quotation of the day," we cannot take either of his positions as true reflections of her own thinking. What we can take, I believe, is a synthesis of the two positions. With her customary love of paradox, Isak Dinesen is able to find a higher truth in the marriage of imitation and intuition by showing, as the story-teller says in "The Blank Page" (LT), that while it is God's story the artist tells (imitates), "the very first germ of a story will come from some mystical place outside the story itself."

This mystical place outside the story is the artist's intuition. It is this intuition that perceives but does not create the story it tells. "For as the hart panteth after the water brook, so panteth the soul of the artist after his motif," says the artist

Cazotte in "Ehrengard." "And who knows whether the motif does not long for that work of art in which it is to be made its true self." As I see it, the soul of the artist (intuition) pants after its motif (God's story—Logos) as the hart pants after the water brook, which both reflects and nourishes. In "The Dreamers" (SGT) Lincoln Forsner, a storyteller in his own right, says to Mira Jama, the archetype of storytellers: "For if you will create, as you know, Mira, you must first imagine."

In a sense, then, the artist is chosen since Isak Dinesen suggests no way that he can come by the possession of a creative imagination other than by having it bestowed upon him. However, being chosen and believing one is chosen are two very different things. This difference is made clear in "Alkmene" (WT), in which Parson Jens Jespersen, who dreamed as a student of becoming a poet and even wrote an epic, failed in his dream when he came to think of himself as having been handpicked by God for some grand purpose. "And it came to this with me:" he tells the young heir to the local manor, Vilhelm, "that I firmly believed myself to have been chosen by the Lord for great things: yes, I held that in the whole world all was done by the Lord with a view to my soul and my destiny. . . . It was a good thing that my condition became clear to me before it was too late. I saw, with great fear, that I was on the brink of the abyss of insanity, and that I must save myself at any cost, at the cost of my studies."

The greatest danger, then, in the belief that one has been specially chosen is that one loses the power of discrimination and finally of action itself. Everything that happens is interpreted as being fraught with meaning for oneself, whether it be there or not; and the significance of whatever meaning really is there is exaggerated. To think as Pastor Jespersen did is to strike one's own bargain, dictate one's own terms, and expect God to comply. But God, as Isak Dinesen envisions him, is not complaisant. His covenant has already been made, and it is man's job to learn His terms and abide by them. Once the artist has ceased to presume and has proudly humbled himself before a greater imagination, he is free to be inspired by that imagination.

Isak Dinesen believes firmly in inspiration as the transmission of the will of God to the artist by means of the Holy Ghost. In "The Deluge at Norderney" she implies that art is the book of the Holy Ghost, and in "The Cardinal's First Tale" (LT) she describes the Holy Ghost as the sire of the artist. "I am not blaspheming, Madame," Cardinal Salviati tells the lady in black, "when I express the idea that any young mother of a saint or great artist may feel herself to be the spouse of the Holy Ghost."

In an essay on Isak Dinesen, Curtis Cate speaks of her storytelling instinct as undoubtedly a Heaven-sent gift of grace and then says: "Isak Dinesen knows as well as anyone that a storyteller must be prepared to sweat blood, and that he must work at his tale as the painter works at his canvas or the potter at his clay. But if there is one divinity she would be ready to enthrone above all others it is Inspiration."[6] And it is the awareness of the possibility of inspiration that, I think, both humbles the artist and makes him proud.

---

6. "Isak Dinesen: The Scheherazade of Our Times," *Cornhill Magazine* (Winter 1959-60), p. 122.

5

THE EXALTED SPIRIT

In *Shadows on the Grass* Isak Dinesen writes: "At times I believe that my feet have been set upon a road which I shall go on following, and that slowly the centre of gravity of my being will shift over from the world of day, from the domain of organizing and regulating universal powers, into the world of Imagination."[1] The artist whose feet "have been set upon a road" is the one who, without faith and without hope, submits to the idea God had when He created him and takes pride in that idea. And when he enters into the world of imagination, he is in tune with God's Logos and ready to function as God's mouthpiece. Cardinal Salviati says, in "The Cardinal's First Tale" (LT): "Yet the Lord indemnifies his mouthpiece. If he is without potency, he has been given a small bit of omnipotence."

In two tales Isak Dinesen indicates what this small bit of omnipotence might include, and there is evidence to support

---

1. P. 112. This statement bears a striking resemblance to the following passage from the *Monologen* of Schleiermacher, who had a profound influence on German Romanticism: " 'Whenever I gaze upon my inward self, I am immediately in the realms of eternity. I behold the activity of the spirit which no world can change, which time cannot destroy, which itself creates both world and time.' " (Trans. Oskar Walzel, *German Romanticism*, New York, 1965, p. 50.)

these two indications in various other tales. In one place she speaks of the "plastic unity of the exalted spirit" to describe the mind in which all opposites have been resolved. In another place she uses the expression "divine swank" to describe the technique and ingenuity of creating the incredible. Both are examples of the indemnification which God grants his mouthpiece.

In "Ehrengard" Cazotte, the artist, says: "But there are natures of such rare nobility that with them no quality nor condition will ever be negative. Incorporated in such a mind anything partakes in its soundness and purity. To the plastic unity of an exalted spirit no conflict exists, but nature and ideal are one. Idea and action, too, are one, inasmuch as the idea is an action and the action an idea." It is just such rare nobility of mind that enables Babette, that culinary virtuoso of "Babette's Feast" (AD), to combine idea and action into a triumphant banquet for a group of pious ascetics in a small Norwegian fishing village. An exile from France, Babette refuses to find anything negative about the frugal conditions under which she is forced to live. She splits cod and makes beer soup with the same care with which she later prepares *cailles en sarcophage* and turtle soup. And under the influence of her rare feast, the elderly religious assembly is rejuvenated and flushed with a joy that lifts them to the essence of their humanity.

Nature and ideal become one as a result of Babette's artistry, but it is a reconciliation of which only she is truly and fully aware. "I shall never be poor," she tells the two elderly sisters who employ her and who know that she has spent her entire fortune on this feast. "I told you that I am a great artist. A great artist, Mesdames, is never poor. We have something, Mesdames, of which other people know nothing."

The split between nature and ideal, between ide[?] action, occurs in the mind of the artist when h[?] conditions as negative, when the plastic unity fa[?] the exalted spirit is deflated by disloyalty and co[?]

violated by the specious praise of the ignorant. " 'It is terrible and unbearable to an artist,' " Babette quotes the artist Papin as saying, " 'to be encouraged to do, to be applauded for doing, his second best.' He said: 'Through all the world there goes one long cry from the heart of the artist: Give me leave to do my utmost!' "

This split also occurs in the spirit of the artist who is threatened by bourgeois fears and restrictions to which he refuses to capitulate. Such is the fate of the child Jens in "The Dreaming Child" (WT). Born under depressing circumstances, Jens clings to a dream which can never be fulfilled amidst the comfortable but restrictive atmosphere of the good people who adopt him. "Within the brotherhood of poets," says the author, "Jens was a humorist, a comic fabulist. It was, in each individual phenomenon of life, the whimsical, the burlesque moment that attracted and inspired him." Emilie, his foster mother, is "distressed by a feeling of impotence which sometimes in the night made her wring her hands." She is impotent because "all her life she had endeavored to separate good from bad, right from wrong, happiness from unhappiness."

Such separations as these are foreign to the unified spirit of the artist, and forced to survive among people who, with the best intentions, struggle to make such distinctions, the unfledged artist can only, as did Jens, wither up and die. Given time, Emilie might have come to understand the lesson of the artist, but Jens is too small to articulate his feelings, and Emilie is too strong for him. It is her lack of understanding that kills him. "Here she was, she reflected with dismay, in the hands of a being, much smaller and weaker than herself, to whom these [good and bad, right and wrong, happiness and unhappiness] were all one, who welcomed light and darkness, pleasure and pain, in the same spirit of gallant, debonair approval and fellowship."

Emilie and her husband do not live up to the expectations of Jens's dream. As a mature poet, Jens would have found satisfaction in turning dream into art, the reality of which, as Cazotte says in "Ehrengard," is "superior to that of the material world." Isak Dinesen sees a parallel between dreams and stories, and in such tales as "The Dreaming Child" and "The Dreamers" (WT) she implies that the artist who is in the hands of a story is not unlike the dreamer in the hands of a dream. The story takes possession of the artist just as the dream takes possession of the dreamer, and it is the artist's job, not to explain the story or make it literal, but to transmit the story and preserve its own reality. It is not the dream-come-true but the dream-become-art that would have saved Jens.

To Isak Dinesen, says Johannes Rosendahl, the artist is the same as the dreamer, and both "are in contact with a 'higher reality.' "[2] Aage Henriksen agrees, and sees this mystical connection, this contact with a "higher reality," in terms of Jung and his theory of the God-like child. He asserts this in an essay devoted to "The Dreaming Child" in which he sees the child Jens as the personification of the Jungian subconscious, and he feels that this explains why the child is never brought to maturity. It is important, says Henriksen, that we see Jens as an essence, an archetype, for he is more poetic spirit than poet.[3]

To turn dream into art, therefore, is to be loyal to the story, not to try to penetrate its mysteries as the classicist does who longs to "understand" what it is he is doing and why. It is just such a classicist that Mira Jama in "The Dreamers" becomes after a long life of telling stories. "When you know what things are really like," he says, "you can make no poems about them. . . . I have become too familiar with life; it can no longer delude me into believing that one thing is much worse than the other. . . . How can you make others afraid when you have forgotten fear yourself?" It is just such "understanding" that shatters the artist's sense of unity and reduces his perspective to one dimension. Nature and ideal have split, and idea has become divorced from action. The dreaming

---

2. *Karen Blixen: Fire Foredrag* (Copenhagen, 1957), p. 26.
3. *Guder og galgefugle* (Oslo, 1956), pp. 29-41.

child has become the old man to whom the world has become literal.

"Now I am on my way down a little," says Mira Jama. "But the tales which I made—they shall last." They shall last, of course, because they are a reflection of that same unbelievable inventiveness which God displayed when he created the world. The artist shares this inventiveness when his spirit is exalted and he is able, like God, to create the incredible and make it fully as acceptable as the astonishing, "unbelievable" world around us. He does this, as God does, by showing how arbitrary reality really is.

When Cazotte, the artist in "Ehrengard," seduces "an old earthenware pot and two lemons into yielding their inmost being" to him, he is doing something as arbitrary and incredible, and yet as "real," as when God compels the acorn to yield Him the oak tree. In performing such deeds, both God and the artist are exercising what Isak Dinesen calls "divine swank."

The valet disguised as a cardinal in "The Deluge at Norderney" (SGT) says to Miss Nat-og-Dag: "Madame, to my mind there never was a great artist who was not a bit of a charlatan; nor a great king, nor a God. The quality of charlatanry is indispensable in a court, or a theater, or in paradise. Thunder and lightning, the new moon, a nightingale, a young girl—all these are bits of charlatanry, of a divine swank." Louis Grandjean finds the same idea present in "Sorrow-Acre" (WT) where "we are given to understand that there is neither a nobleman nor a God without charlatanry or the technique of impressing people."[4]

The label of "seducer" is applied to the artist by the Countess von Gassner, who is the great-grandmother of the storyteller of "Ehrengard." Writing a letter in reply to this, Cazotte says:

You call an artist a seducer and are not aware that you are paying him the highest of compliments. The whole attitude of the artist

---

4. *Blixens Animus* (Copenhagen, 1957), p. 36.

towards the Universe is that of a seducer. For what does seduction mean but the ability to make, with infinite trouble, patience and perseverance, the object upon which you concentrate your mind give forth, voluntarily and enraptured, its very core and essence? Aye, and to reach, in the process, a higher beauty than it could ever, under any other circumstances, have attained?

Seduction such as Cazotte describes depends upon the willing cooperation of the object to be seduced. In such willingness lies the secret of the creation. It is essential that the object cooperate in its seduction, that it be approached in such a way that it will surrender its essence voluntarily and enraptured. In this way only will the essence yield itself inviolate.

Cazotte is very much aware of the pains that must be taken before the prize can be extracted, for every object has its own fragile essence which can only be got at with delicacy. He makes this clear in his letter to the countess: "But do not imagine, wise and sagacious Mama, that the seducer's art must in each individual engagement fetch him the same trophy. There are women who give out the fullness of their womanhood in a smile, a side glance or a waltz, and others who will be giving it in their tears. I may drink off a bottle of Rhine wine to its last drop, but I sip only one glass of a *fine,* and there be rare vintages from which I covet nothing but the bouquet."

As a seducer the artist is not quite respectable, but, then, Isak Dinesen never admired respectability. While in Africa, she and Berkeley Cole classified animals into two groups— those that were decent and those that were respectable—and it was animals like the lion and the water buffalo that were decent while domesticated animals like chickens and pigs were respectable.[5] Erik Johannesson has noted that Isak Dinesen shares with Thomas Mann the view that the artist is, in a way, a confidence man because "he does not mirror reality; he transforms it, or recreates it, in his imagination."[6]

---

5. *Shadows on the Grass,* pp. 17-18.
6. *The World of Isak Dinesen* (Seattle, 1961), p. 76.

This is, of course, what divine swank is all about—the trans-
forming of reality in the imagination. "The greatest of his
art," Johannesson adds, in interpretation of this idea, "depends on the courage and the range of his imagination."[7]
And the courage and range of the imagination depend, as I
interpret Isak Dinesen, on how completely the artist has
achieved the plastic unity of the exalted spirit.

7. Ibid.

6

THE MEASURE OF DISTRESS

SPEAKING OF the artist, Cardinal Salviati in "The Cardinal's First Tale" (LT) says to the lady in black: "Pity him not, this man. Doomed he will be, it is true, and forever lonely, and wherever he goes his commission will be that of breaking hearts, because the sacrifice of God is a broken and contrite heart." The cardinal then goes on to explain how God compensates the artist by giving him a bit of omnipotence. We have already seen how this bit of omnipotence manifests itself through the exalted spirit. In this chapter we shall see to what extent the artist's own heart can be broken and made contrite.

In the tales of Isak Dinesen, the artist is the consort of loneliness and longing and is excluded from the society of common humanity in that he cannot enjoy the benefits either of honor or of remorse. Denied most of the prerogatives of either God or the devil, he is forced, nevertheless, as a man, to wear their immortal masks in a theatrical that lacks even the dignity of tragedy. As we shall see when we come to a discussion of her concept of comedy and tragedy, Isak Dinesen holds that those who function on this earth in lieu of God (artist, priest, aristocrat) can never be truly tragic figures. Tragedy is the privilege of ordinary mortals alone, and the gods and

their agents must never condescend to be pitied; for to pity
them is to annihilate them, as the old lord explains in "Sorrow-
Acre" (WT).

The suffering of the artist is in proportion to the demands
of his art. "I will not measure you out any more distress than
you need to write your books," says the Lord to Charlie Despard in "The Young Man with the Carnation" (WT). "For,"
He adds, "it is I who want them written." Not inscrutable
fate, then, nor blind chance, but God's deliberate intervention
seals the artist's doom. For this reason the artist is forbidden
from thinking of his suffering as excessive or pitiable.

The first distress which is measured out to Despard is
that of longing. When he announces to the Lord that he is
going to write a love story, the Lord asks him if it is to be
"a great and sweet tale, which will live in the hearts of young
lovers." Despard says that it is to be such a story, indeed, and
the Lord asks: "And are you content with that?" Charlie is
dismayed. "O Lord, what are you asking me? How can I
answer yes? Am I not a human being, and can I write a love
story without longing for that love which clings and embraces,
and for the softness and warmth of a young woman's body
in my arms?"

The Lord explains that it was Despard himself who made
the choice, who jumped out of a woman's bed to pursue that
glimpse of a lost involvement with life which he had observed
in the face of the young man with the carnation. That, the
Lord implies, was the moment of choice, and it was Despard's
own choice, but he cannot have it both ways. Either he could
remain with the woman and be one with common humanity,
or he could abandon her in favor of the love story about her.
This is not a choice that Despard finds easy to accept, even
though it is his own. "Nay, tell me, now that we are at it,"
he says to the Lord, "am I, while I write of the beauty of young
women, to get, from the live women of the earth, a shilling's
worth, and no more?" "Yes," the Lord replies. "And you are
to be content with that."

Robert Langbaum sees Despard's choice between the

real and the imaginary as one which Isak Dinesen considers unavoidable to the artist. "It is because the artist does not 'live,' " says Langbaum, "is physically impotent and sterile, that he lives so strongly in the imagination as to give life to other people through an overflow of imaginative energy. The artist is in this sense like God who does not share in the warm flesh-and-blood life. He creates."[1]

When Charlie Despard reappears at the end of *Winter's Tales* in "A Consolatory Tale," he has apparently come to terms with his choice. In this story he makes oblique reference to the dialogue that took place between him and the Lord in the earlier story. That earlier dialogue had concluded in the manner of the story of Job with the Lord speaking, as it were, in a whirlwind and explaining through a series of questions that the answer to why Despard must be content with longing lay in God's omnipotence and was not to be understood in any other way. In "A Consolatory Tale" Despard says to the storyteller Aeneas Snell: "The Lord in the whirlwind pleads the defense of the artist, and of the artist only."

If, as it has already been pointed out, Despard sees the artist in the role of God and the public as Job, then it is not difficult to see why the voice in the whirlwind appeases Despard. As an artist he knows that the demands of the reader for explanation and clarification cannot always be met. The explanation of creation is creation itself, and a great imagination is its own defense.

Longing means more to Isak Dinesen than just a desire for involvement with the objects with which the artist deals. Denied the pleasures of ordinary human intercourse, the artist can find compensation in the creation of works of art; but there is a longing of the sort that leads beyond human existence and which can only be described in terms of a longing for a union with God, a oneness with the essence of creation. The poet Johannes Ewald betrays this sort of longing in "Converse at Night in Copenhagen" (LT) when he expresses the desire to work out his Mythos from the divine Logos of God.

---

1. *The Gayety of Vision* (New York, 1965), p. 16.

We can see something of the nature of the two types of longing and of their relationship to each other in the tale "The Dreaming Child" (WT). Of Jens, the archetypal God-like child, the author says:

He was not at all a person to be permanently set at ease by what the world calls fortune. The essence of his nature was longing. The warm rooms with silk curtains, the sweets, his toys and new clothes, the kindness and concern of his Papa and Mamma were all of the greatest moment because they went to prove the veracity of his visions; they were infinitely valuable as embodiments of his dreams. But within themselves they hardly meant anything to him, and they had no power to hold him. He was neither a worldling nor a struggler. He was a Poet.

Johannes Rosendahl compares this story to "The Poet" (SGT) and says that in both tales Isak Dinesen "gives the poet who is not capable of living . . . the ability to see the mystical connections of existence."[2]

Throughout her tales Isak Dinesen reminds us that whenever an artist steps into the real world and attempts to turn dreams into reality, he fails. Such is Cazotte's fate in "Ehrengard," and Mathiesen's in "The Poet," and such also is Jens's fate when he is adopted by his longed-for foster parents. The fulfillment of his dreams proves to Jens the "veracity of his visions," but it also proves to him that he can be no part of that fulfillment. If he were older, he might, as Despard says of himself in comparable circumstances, "sit in a room and write down these words, to be praised by the critics, while outside, in the corridor, ran the road of the young man with the carnation into that light which made his face shine." He cannot have both, and for the true artist there is no choice.

To the lady in black who feels sorry for the artist, Cardinal Salviati, who has already warned her not to feel pity, says this: "But if indeed . . . your kind heart yearns to melt in compassion, I may tell you at the same time, that to this chosen officeholder of the Lord—so highly favored in many things—certain spiritual benefits, granted to other human

2. *Karen Blixen: Fire Foredrag* (Copenhagen, 1957), p. 26.

beings, are indeed withheld."[3] "Of what benefits are you speaking?" the lady in black asks, and the cardinal replies: "I am speaking of the benefit of remorse. To the man of whom we speak it is forbidden. The tears of repentance, in which the souls of nations are blissfully cleansed, are not for him. Quod fecit, fecit!"

Whatever is done, is done! The oath has been taken and the risk run. There is no room for regret. When Charlie Despard asks for assurances of God's covenant, God says: "You will not be certain of it at all times. But I tell you now that it is so. You will have to hold on to that." I have speculated elsewhere about Isak Dinesen's reasons for believing that the artist must ever doubt his calling, and I think it is clear here that without the benefit of remorse, the artist is even less likely to take his role lightly or for granted. Obviously, the consequences of overconfidence are doubly disastrous if the guilty artist is denied repentance as well as reward.

Kuno Poulsen conjectures rather interestingly about the idea of remorselessness as a necessary attribute of the artist. In an essay entitled "Karen Blixens gamle og nye Testamente" ("Karen Blixen's Old and New Testament"), Poulsen differentiates two significant motifs in her works and relates them both to the concerns of her characters and to her concerns about the artist.[4] He maintains that Isak Dinesen resolves the conflicting but equally important questions of identity and metamorphosis by assigning them complementary functions in the make-up of the artist. The question Who am I? (What is my role? What is my mask? What is my duty?) is, as he sees it, her equivalent of the Old Testament where the question of identity is paramount. With the coming of Christ and the metamorphosis of God into man, the question of change becomes

---

3. From the explanation that precedes this statement, in which the cardinal makes it clear that the artist "was neither forced or lured into service," it is to be understood that the word "chosen" in this context means one who has petitioned to take the oath and not one whom God has singled out for great things.

4. *Vindrosen*, X (1963), no. 5, p. 379.

paramount. Not Who am I? but What can I become? Not
What is? but What can be? The question is answered by turning the passivity of identity into the activity of change—by
becoming. And with such a forward step there can be no turning back, no regret, no remorse. It is by virtue of this assertion
of remorselessness, says Poulsen, that Isak Dinesen's idea of
metamorphosis parallels the New Testament of Christianity.[5]

Another benefit that is withheld from the artist, one which
the cardinal does not mention but which is explained by an
artist in "Copenhagen Season" (LT), is the benefit of honor.
Honor, as Isak Dinesen explains it through the character of
the artist in this tale, belongs entirely to man and came about
as a result of the Fall of Man, the loss of paradise, and the
subsequent awareness of shame. Her definition of honor, as I
see it, is the wish on the part of man to regain his dignity before God—or, as the artist puts it, to regain his naiveté.

Remorse, the child of shame, is the basis of honor; and
since the artist is denied remorse, he has no need for honor.
However, he values the idea of honor because it is the basis
for tragedy, which he can imitate artistically but which he
cannot experience personally. "I will not exchange the idea
of honor for a flying ticket to the moon," says the artist. "I am
an artist, I have no honor of my own, and can yet speak with
connoisseurship about honor. In Paradise there was no idea of
honor. ('And they saw that they were naked'—that comes in
later, and would by no means have been an objectionable sight
to the eye of an artist.) And I thank God that the people whose
portraits I paint have still in their hearts the idea of honor, by
which tragedy is created."

The artist is like a third observer of the events in Eden.
God is concerned with transgression, Satan with blind obedi-
ence, and the artist with shame. Just as God cannot transgress,
nor Satan obey, the artist cannot know shame. All three ob-
serve what they cannot experience. As a spectator, then, the
artist cannot share with the transgressors the luxury of their

5. Ibid. p. 379.

proud sorrow and contrition—their remorse. Instead, along with God, the punisher, and Satan, the tempter, he must stand aloof and tell the story.

No one feels the loneliness and the longing, the estrangement from common humanity and its spiritual benefits more sensitively than the poet Johannes Ewald, masquerading as Yorick in "Converse at Night in Copenhagen". He reminds young King Christian VII that the two of them, as artist and aristocrat, share a common burden. "Terrible," he says to the king, "is the comprehension of this our obligation toward the Lord. Terrible in its weight and incessancy is the obligation of the acorn to yield Him the Oak tree—and yet it is exquisite, too, and sweet and pleasant in the young verdure after a summer rain." He then turns specifically to the pact which the artist must make with the Lord before he can produce art—the pact in which the Lord offers a bit of omnipotence and a measure of distress in return for the submission of the artist. "Crushing in its weight," says the poet, "is my own covenant with the Lord, yet it is, at the same time, highly gay and glorious! For if I do only hold onto it myself, no adversity and no distress shall compel me, but it is I who shall compel adversity, poverty and sickness, and the harshness even of my enemies, and force those to labor with me for my benefit. And all things shall work together for good to me!"

No quality or condition will ever be negative to the exalted spirit, says the artist in "Ehrengard," and the poet Ewald shows us how the measure of distress which the Lord places upon the artist is made positive by the artist and turned to his advantage. Honor and remorse are irrelevant qualities to the artist; he has no need of them. But adversity and distress, poverty and sickness, even the harshness of his enemies, are the realities of which he is arbiter. Here, if anywhere, can be seen the peculiar power of Isak Dinesen's theory of submission. It is gay and glorious and not the least craven. We get from life, she says in one of her tales, both what we ask for and what we reject. Both are gifts, and the artist, in not separating them, acquires dominion over them.

III

LOGOS AND MYTHOS

7

STORY AND TALE

"IN THE BEGINNING was the story," Cardinal Salviati tells the lady in black in "The Cardinal's First Tale" (LT). "Stories," he explains, "have been told as long as speech has existed, and sans stories the human race would have perished, as it would have perished sans water." The old lord in "Sorrow-Acre" (WT) says to his nephew: "You will have learned in school that in the beginning was the word." Johannes Ewald, the poet in "Converse at Night in Copenhagen" (LT), says to the king: "By the Word all things were created." Thus, a priest, an aristocrat, and a poet all confirm Isak Dinesen's assertion of the primacy of either the Word or the story as the fountainhead of all creation. Because she has used the words "Word" and "story" interchangeably, I am proceeding on the assumption that she thinks of them as one.

The cardinal goes on to call the story the divine art, the old lord calls the Word the principle of the world, and Ewald maintains that God expects the poet to return to Him and bring Him back His Word, as speech. If we examine these various comments, we shall see that, according to Isak Dinesen, art not only derives from the story but actually is the story properly defined.

The cardinal begins by according the story a position

before which nothing else can be said to exist. In such a position, and equated, as I assume it is, with the Word, the story can perhaps be defined as the impulse behind or the original idea for art. It can also be said to precede creation of any kind and to contain within itself the ingredients of creation, which, as we shall see, include considerations of value as well as technique.

After establishing the primacy of the story, the cardinal goes on to say that stories have been told as long as speech has existed. A "told" story is, then, as I see it, an original impulse communicated. In this case, the original impulse is communicated through speech. According to Ewald, the Word precedes speech, and speech is the earthly reflection of the Word. Thus, if story means both Word and speech, which I believe it does, this can only lead to confusion unless there is some way of clarifying or justifying what seems to be a contradiction.

Ewald offers just such a way when he uses the Greek words *Logos* and *Mythos*—*Logos* to refer to the Word, and *Mythos* to refer to its earthly reflection. He calls the Logos the creative force, the beginning, and the Mythos the abiding substance, remembrance. When the cardinal uses the term *story,* he is, in effect, referring to the harmony between the creative force (Logos) and the abiding substance (Mythos). In other words, when the Mythos is a true reflection of the Logos, the term *story* can, it seems, properly be applied to both. If this is so, then the story is the way in which, I think, Isak Dinesen would define form. According to this interpretation, art has form when it is a faithful (loyal) representation of the creative force. Art that has such form can be said to be a "story."[1]

The cardinal goes on to compare stories with water as a necessity for survival. Thus, art assumes all the life-giving,

---

1. Because Isak Dinesen uses the terms *story* and *tale* interchangeably it is to be understood that the word *story,* as it appears in this study, means *tale* unless otherwise indicated.

cleansing, and resurrecting qualities of water and is important not just for pleasure or utility but for sheer existence. Such an assertion suggests that art must continue in order to assure mankind's survival, and that such continuation maintains the link with the origin of all things by serving as a collective memory. The cessation of art would mean spiritual death just as the absence of water would mean physical death. In fact, when the cardinal says that the human race would "perish" without stories, he implies both spiritual and physical death. Spiritual death that leads to physical death occurs in some of Isak Dinesen's tales such as "The Poet" (SGT), "The Dreaming Child" (WT), "The Caryatids" (LT), and "The Immortal Story" (AD). This, for her, I think, is true tragedy: the death of the spirit, the loss of art, the severing of the connection with the creative force, the beginning.

The old lord in "Sorrow-Acre" calls this creative force the "principle of our world." I have stated elsewhere his argument with his nephew Adam over principle and law, and I have maintained that principle refers to Logos and law to Mythos. The old lord's confusion of the terms, as when he speaks of the law of gravitation as a principle of our world, is less perplexing in the light of the cardinal's comprehensive use of the word "story." The law of gravitation is really the manifestation of an antecedent principle of gravitation. The old lord is using the terms interchangeably in their ordinary connotation, and this is no crime. The crime comes in ignoring or not seeing the distinction and in thus assuming that law is as dynamic as principle. If law derives from principle, law is subject to principle. Adam insists that the Word (the principle) is creative and, therefore, superior to restricting and controlling laws. The outcome of the argument between Adam and his uncle is an affirmation of the ceaseless energy of the Word. Thus, the Word is not only primary but dynamic.

Ewald reaffirms the primary and dynamic qualities of the Word and adds to these the quality of ominpotence. "By the word *all* things were created," he says (emphasis mine), and goes on to specify the way in which the Word manifests itself through the artist. Through his precise use of the words Logos and Mythos, Ewald makes clear to us the connection between creative force and all creation; and by defining the terms under which the artist works, he suggests that the Word is not only primary and dynamic but also ultimate. "At the moment when my Almighty Father first created me by his word, he demanded and expected from me that I should one day return to Him and bring Him back His word, as speech. . . . And in time to come," he adds, "when by His infinite grace I shall once more have become one with Him, then will we look down together from heaven—I myself with tears, but my God with a smile—demanding and expecting that this mythos of mine shall remain after me on earth."

The Mythos that remains on earth, after the artist, is, of course, his art; and Isak Dinesen has provided sufficient clues throughout her tales to give us a fairly accurate, if not comprehensive, idea of what she considers to be the major ingredients of a work of art. Usually what she says can be liberally applied to any art, but her criticism is directed primarily towards the literary arts, and particularly the art of the tale. Therefore, it is with the tale in mind that this analysis is presented, but it is assumed that her principles generally hold true for other art forms. It is fitting, then, before beginning a discussion of the ingredients of art, to take a closer look at her attitude toward the tale.

The most obvious reason why Isak Dinesen speaks more explicitly about the tale than about any other art form is that she was herself a writer—and a teller—of tales. She would probably not like for us to say that she chose the tale, or even that it chose her. She would probably prefer to call it a love affair, the ecstatic union of the destined with his destiny. While in Africa she rediscovered the ancient and venerable tradition of storytelling in its pristine state. As a young girl, she had enjoyed telling stories to members of her family; and among her fondest childhood recollections were the hours she spent wandering over the hills around Rungstedlund listening to the tales her father had brought back from his sojourn among the Indians in Wisconsin. When she began to tell stories to the natives on her farm in Kenya, she came to understand how very important the story was to them. They were also a wisely critical audience, and it was from the experience of telling them stories and gauging their reactions that, I would surmise, she derived her sensitive understanding of the complex and subtle relationship between the artist and his audience. Years later, when she was an established writer, she enjoyed recording tales or reciting them before television audiences both in Denmark and the United States. It was always the oral tradition that she preferred.

But she knew the limitations of the oral tradition, and she surpassed them when she began putting stories on paper. Her written tales are complex and highly polished and do not lend themselves easily to recitation in their entirety. Whenever she was asked to read them, she usually chose inset stories with the simple, direct action and sharp, ironic insight that characterize the oral tale.

Aside from personal preference, she revered the tale as a pure and original genre. She saw in it, I believe, an unbroken link with man's prehistoric beginnings. By reminding us, as she does so often, that in the beginning was the story and that stories have always been *told,* she is, in effect, placing the tale first in the ranks of literature and on a level with those art forms which anthropologists have traced to prehistory and which they have designated as spontaneous, archetypal expression—dance, music, drawing.

Isak Dinesen tried her hand at just about every literary genre—drama, poetry, novel, essay; but it would be foolish to say that she returned to the tale because she thought it superior. She returned to it, without a doubt, because she excelled at it. However, her ventures into other genres, although not extensive and only moderately successful, do allow her to speak about them with some authority. Unfor-

tunately, she has little to say about any type other than the
novel. There is plenty of evidence to prove her love for poetry
and drama, but beyond mere admiration for these genres, she
has given us little critical commentary of any value. If the
age and endurance of a genre have the meaning for her that
I have suggested, then it would be safe to assume that she
would rank poetry and drama just slightly below the tale.[2]

About the novel, however, she does have something to
say, and what she says is not always flattering. Her admiration for Cervantes is admiration for a teller of tales which
are built around a unifying element. In *Don Quixote* it is the
action that she regards as more important than the character,
for she makes it quite clear that character should be subordinate to plot. I intend to develop this important point exten-
sively in the following chapter. However, what she has to
say about the novel as an inferior literary genre is pertinent
to this discussion of the supremacy of the tale.

Cardinal Salviati in "The Cardinal's First Tale," speaking two centuries ago, says to the lady in black: "I see, today,
a new art of narration, a novel literature and category of
belles-lettres, dawning upon the world. It is, indeed, already
with us, and it has gained great favor amongst the readers
of our time. And this new art and literature—for the sake
of the individual characters in the story, and in order to keep
close to them and not be afraid—will be ready to sacrifice
the story itself." He goes on to argue that the characters of
novels are so close to the reader that the story gets neglected.
He then says: "The literature of which we are speaking—the
literature of individuals, if we may call it so—is a noble art,
a great, earnest, and ambitious human product. But it is a
human product. The divine art is the story. In the beginning
was the story."

---

2. I submit that she respects Homer as a teller of tales first and a poet
second, and that she considers the epic a loosely organized accumulation
of tales about a common subject. At the time of her death, she was at
work on a collection of tales to be called *Albondocani,* which was to
have contained one hundred separate tales all related to a common
theme.

This reaffirmation of the primacy of the story and the relegation of the novel to an inferior status is based, apparently, on Isak Dinesen's objection to the sacrificing of everything to character. Mythos, after all, also means "plot"—and if form is achieved through the reflection of the Logos in the Mythos, then everything, she seems to be saying, is subordinated to plot. In stating that the human product is the "literature of individuals," Isak Dinesen is excluding from serious consideration as art any literary form that elevates character above everything else. Without subordination of character, none of her other critical principles can reasonably be applied.

Isak Dinesen's veneration of the tale has its mystical reasons, too. Charlie Despard, her counterpart, in "The Young Man with the Carnation" (WT), says "from the bottom of his heart": "Almighty God, as the heavens are higher than the earth, so are thy short stories higher than our short stories." To Isak Dinesen, God is not a painter or a poet or a musician. He is above all a teller of tales. *The* divine art is the story, the primary pattern of all art. Creation is a story, and we are told this story step by step, as the story progresses. There is a beginning and a middle and an end (the seventh day), and the characters appear in the story on a given day.

It is the unfolding that is important to Isak Dinesen. What matters is not what happens to man so much as the way in which it happens. It is only in the working out of the story that all men participate. There can be no story without man, yet man is subordinate to the story. Man and his destiny are the dancer and the dance, and I think Isak Dinesen believed that this inevitable fusion is best conveyed through the story because the story is the most comprehensive art form both in terms of what it can include and in terms of whom it reaches. But it is also superior because it is the way in which the story of creation has been unfolded to man. As the means whereby creation is unfolded, the story, it seems, is the artistic counterpart of creation, and the other art forms are but parts of this greater art.

The elevation of the tale to the highest art form is a
departure from the romantic tendency to exalt music above
all other art, but Isak Dinesen still shares with E. T. A.
Hoffmann, with whom she has much else in common, the
romantic fondness for using musicians as serious subjects for
literary treatment—even if she does not share his reverence
for them. It is interesting to note, however, that the one
character in her tales who bears the most obvious resemblance
to herself is Pellegrina Leoni, a renowned opera singer.[3] In
"The Dreamers" (WT), the first story in which Pellegrina
Leoni appears, her identity is deliberately confused as she
moves in and out of the story in a succession of widely vary-
ing disguises. One purpose of the story seems to be an attempt
to show that the personality takes on meaning only in the
context of the role it is playing—when, in other words, character is subordinate to plot.

3. Kuno Poulsen, "Karen Blixens gamle og nye Testamente," *Vindrosen*,
X (1963), no. 5, pp. 377-379.

8

QUESTIONS OF VALUE
(Truth, Reality, and Order)

Isak Dinesen is concerned primarily with judging a work of art as a unique manifestation of its own inner law. She once said to an interviewer: "People are always asking me what is the significance of this or that in the tales—'What does this symbolize? What does that stand for?' and I always have a difficult time making them believe that I intend everything as it's stated. It would be terrible if the explanation of the work were outside the work itself."[1]

What she is saying, of course, is that art has its own rationale, that it conforms to no standards but the ones it imposes upon itself, and these vary from one work of art to another. She avoids artistic anarchy, I think, by the restrictions she places upon the artist. These restrictions, as we have seen in the preceding section, will incline the artist towards that mode of expression proper for him and will impose upon him the necessity of seeking constant assurance that he is doing what his destiny has assigned him. Through submission to a greater imagination, Isak Dinesen assumes that the artist will strive to reflect the divine Logos in his human art. Thus, the standards which he brings to bear on that art will, hopefully,

---

1. Eugene Walter, "Isak Dinesen" (interview *Paris Review* [Autumn 1956]) p. 56.

conform to those which inspired it. The rules, therefore, are not of the artist's making, but of God's. Whether or not the artist is successful, depends, of course, upon the ultimate effect of the work of art on its audience, for this audience response is the test of the artist's loyalty to the Logos. We shall see in the next section how concerned Isak Dinesen is that the audience should understand its obligations and know how to evaluate its reactions.

Although Isak Dinesen does not attempt to specify what should or should not be included in a work, she does concern herself with a number of things which she finds common to most works and about which there is often a great deal of misunderstanding. These common properties fall into the categories of questions of value and questions of technique. Questions of value concern matters of truth, reality, and order; questions of technique concern matters of character, distance, and distortion. While not exhaustive, these matters are the ones which she is specifically interested in. Her chief concern, I feel, is that a work of art be appreciated on the basis of what its intrinsic nature demands of it and not on the basis of arbitrarily imposed rules that do not allow for what might be called "improvisation."[2]

Rules, in other words, derive from the work of art which they are evaluating and are, therefore, relative. They are not distilled absolutes that can be deduced and applied indiscriminately. The matters dealt with here are matters that Isak Dinesen discusses because they are the ones that I think she would say are most subject to "improvisation" within a work of art.

For example, a preconceived idea of what constitutes truth or reality or order might easily prevent a critic from recognizing a conscious disregard for such conventions. In the case of truth, Isak Dinesen asks, not that it be present or absent in a work, but whether or not its presence or absence matters.

---

2. This is my own term, and I have introduced it only to suggest that the presence in a work of art of the values under discussion does not define their use.

In "The Deluge at Norderney" (SGT), Miss Malin Nat-og-Dag, that remarkably shrewd woman of wisdom and experience, says in a tone of surprise to the valet who is disguised as a cardinal: "Where in all the world did you get the idea that the Lord wants the truth from us? It is a strange, a most original, idea of yours, My Lord. Why, he knows it already, and may even have found it a little bit dull. Truth is for tailors and shoemakers, My Lord. I, on the contrary, have always held that the Lord has a penchant for masquerades." This is a reference, no doubt, to God's masquerading as Christ, a point made not only in this story but also in "The Fish" (WT). The truth lies not in God *or* Christ, it seems, but in God *and* Christ; and the mask, which is commonly thought to conceal truth, actually passes for it by showing us the oneness of opposites.

Isak Dinesen does not define truth in terms of physical or psychological realism, or puzzles solved and questions answered. These are the things God knows already, and whether or not they are really truth, we commonly accept them as truth and, Isak Dinesen implies in the statement just quoted, waste our time boring God with our knowledge of them. What God wants, Miss Malin suggests, is our cooperation in the masquerade, not our misguided attempts to tell Him and each other how things really are. How is this possible when, in the first place, we can never be sure we know how things really are? "I should never have the courage to paint a rose as it looks," says Count Augustus von Schimmelmann in "The Poet" (SGT). "For how does a rose look?"

The job of the artist is to turn reality into masquerade once he has perceived the masquerade behind reality. Reality is at the farthest extreme from truth, with the mask in between. When we move from reality to mask, we move closer to truth, but we do not perceive truth until God deigns to lower the mask. If, as the valet/cardinal says, it is the Lord who will unmask Himself at the stroke of midnight, the day of judgment, then it is from Him we are to expect truth, not from the artist. Artistic truth, therefore, lies not in some transient con-

ception of what really is but in the fidelity with which the
Mythos reflects the Logos and makes perceptible the otherwise imperceptible mask of God. "The reality of Art [is] superior to that of the material world," says the artist Cazotte in
"Ehrengard"; therefore, it must obviously be different from
the reality of the material world.

The young Count Augustus von Schimmelmann in "The
Roads Round Pisa" (SGT) speculates about the difficulty of
knowing the truth and thinks that a mirror tells you the truth
about yourself. He has changed his mind by the time he reappears in "The Poet,"[3] but even in "The Roads Round Pisa"
he betrays doubt when he recalls a visit to the Panoptikon in
Copenhagen where he saw himself reflected in hundreds of
variously curved mirrors and recognized in the distortions of
his reflections "how much this was like real life. So your own
self," he thinks, "your personality and existence are reflected
within the mind of each of the people whom you meet and live
with, into a likeness, a caricature of yourself, which still lives
on and pretends to be, in some way, the truth about you."

Erik Johannesson compares Isak Dinesen with Yeats, for
whom "the contemplation of the self is seen as a source of
passivity and melancholy."[4] Both prefer masks, and their use
of masks, he says, "is deeply rooted in a genuine sense for the
multiple possibilities of the self."[5] "Not by the face shall the
man be known," says the valet/cardinal, "but by the mask."
Isak Dinesen, like Yeats, says Johannesson, "regards the
adoption of a mask as an active, passionate, and self-master-
ing state, making for greatness. . . . To don a mask is regarded
as an aristocratic manner: to play the lover, the hero, the saint,
requires the aristocratic virtues of courage and imagination,
and a passionate affirmation of destiny."[6] Aristocratic and
artistic virtues are very similar in Isak Dinesen's thinking, and

---

3. Cf. Part II, chap. 2, pp. 38-39.
4. "Isak Dinesen, Søren Kierkegaard, and the Present Age," *Books Abroad,*
   XXXV (1962), no. 1, 20-21.
5. Ibid., p. 20.
6. Ibid., p. 21.

Johannesson believes that her insistence on mask play is a defense of the aristocratic virtues against the bourgeois virtues of sincerity, security, and being true to one's own self.[7]

Hans Brix takes Isak Dinesen to task for violating physical realism.[8] If she does violate physical realism, it is apparently because she feels that the artist obeys spiritual rather than natural laws. Her settings and characters are idealized; they are seen not through the distortion of a mirror but through the perception of a mind which orders things to conform with the dictates of a higher reality—a higher imagination. They are, in a word, dreamlike in that they seem to have had an existence even though they could never really have existed.

The relationship between art and dream figures importantly in Isak Dinesen's attitude toward reality. In *Shadows on the Grass* she writes: "For we have in the dream forsaken our allegiance to the organizing, controlling and rectifying forces of the world, the Universal Conscience. We have sworn fealty to the wild, incalculable, creative forces, the Imagination of the Universe,"[9] I think it can be shown that this statement is far from a cry for artistic anarchy. Anarchy lies in the opposite direction from such concepts as identity and metamorphosis, submission and destiny, that we have seen as central to Isak Dinesen's thinking. The organizing, controlling, and rectifying forces mentioned in this passage are simply the bourgeois virtues that Johannesson lists as sincerity, security, and being true to one's own self. These are the ingredients of the universal conscience and have nothing to do with art, which puts the mask above sincerity, uncertainty above security, and loyalty to the story above loyalty to one's self. The wild, incalculable, creative forces are the daring, passion, and imagination of the Word that Adam praises in "Sorrow-Acre" (WT). They are the principle of art, not the law; and when one swears fealty to

7. Ibid. p. 21.
8. *Karen Blixens Eventyr* (Copenhagen, 1949), pp. 125, 214.
9. P. 110.

them, he is yielding to authority, not anarchy—he is being loyal to the story and keeping the ideas of the author clear.

The imagination of the universe is the source of art, not the structure. When, farther on, Isak Dinesen speaks about shifting over "from the world of day, from the domain of organizing and regulating universal powers, into the world of Imagination,"[10] she is talking, I think, about a movement away from bourgeois values toward divine ones. The domain of organizing and regulating universal powers, since it is contrasted with the world of imagination, obviously refers to the sort of worldly reality by which we may mistakenly judge art. The dream can neither be argued nor explained. It must be accepted on its own terms. And if this dream, which derives from the imagination of the universe, is reflected in art, then art must also be accepted on its own terms. This is a plea, I think, not for disorder in art, but for order of a kind different from that of reality.

The order of reality excludes compression and expansion. Every moment is of the same duration as every other, and one moment inexorably follows another. The order of art, like dream, lengthens some moments and shortens others. The relationship of one event to another is dictated by the inner logic of the work and is not bound by chronology. "What particularly pleases me about dreams," says Mira Jama in "The Dreamers" (SGT), "is this: that there the world creates itself around me without any effort on my part." He then goes on to illustrate the way in which a dream follows an order which is totally unlike the order of reality.

"Here, now, if I want to go to Gazi, I have to bargain for a boat, and to buy and pack my provisions, to tack up against the wind, and even to make my hands sore by rowing. And then, when I get to Gazi, what am I to do there? Of that also I must think. But in my dreams I find myself walking up a long row of stone steps which lead from the sea. These steps I have not seen before, yet I feel that to climb them is a great happiness, and that they will take me to something highly enjoyable. Or I find myself hunting

10. Ibid., p. 112.

in a long row of low hills, and I have got people with me with bows and arrows, and dogs in leads. But what I am to hunt, or why I have gone there, I do not know. One time I came into a room from a balcony, in the very early morning, and upon the stone floor stood a woman's two little sandals, and at the same moment I thought: they are hers. And at that my heart overflowed with pleasure, rocked in ease. But I had taken no trouble. I had had no expense to get the woman. And at other times I have been aware that outside the door was a big black man, very black, who meant to kill me; but still I had done nothing to make him my enemy, and I shall just wait for the dream itself to inform me how to escape from him, for in myself I cannot find out how to do it."

The phrase "and I shall just wait for the dream itself to inform me" is important and could apply to any of the unresolved situations in Mira Jama's account. Dream and imagination, as Isak Dinesen describes them, are, it would seem, synonyms for Logos. When this Logos is reflected in the Mythos, all we can expect from the Mythos is fidelity to the Logos (or dream), not complete understanding. The dream will present itself as it wishes to present itself, and will carry whatever explanations it cares to. If it wishes to inform Mira Jama how to escape from the big black man, or what to do once he gets to Gazi, it will—but it is not obliged to. It is reality that likes to deal in explanations, not dream or art. "I will tell you a tale tonight," says Mira Jama to Lincoln Forsner. "I will give you no explanation. You must take in whatever you can, and leave the rest outside. It is not a bad thing in a tale that you can understand only half of it."

What is important to Isak Dinesen, says Johannes Rosendahl, "is whether the audience sees the dream in the work of art or whether it sees only its poor impression."[11] Rosendahl says that Isak Dinesen sees all works of art as created from the ideal beautiful dream. "The ideal dream and the work of art are thus dependent upon each other," he explains. "If the work of art is meritorious, it will proclaim the magnificence of the

---

11. *Karen Blixen: Fire Foredrag* (Copenhagen, 1957), p. 31.

dream. If the dream is magnificent, it will give beauty to the work of art."[12]

Isak Dinesen allows that dreams may have nightmarish qualities, but she does not believe that there is a place for nightmare as ultimate vision in art. "Our beautiful dreams," she writes, "are not confined to the spheres of the idyll or the child's play, or to any such sphere as in the life of day-time is considered safe or pleasant. Horrible events take place in them, monsters appear, abysses open, wild turbulent flights and pursuits are familiar features of theirs. Only, on entering their world, horror changes hue. Monstrosity and monsters, Hell itself—they turn to favour and to prettiness."[13] According to this statement, nightmare would have to be defined as a dream in which horror remains horror. Her remark, however, does not allow for nightmare as a total dream. For her, apparently, horror always changes hue, and nightmare can only be a partial vision. Therefore, we must conclude that to call a dream a nightmare is to distort the dream. If she does think of nightmare as an unfinished or unresolved bad dream, then we can understand why she feels free to exclude it from the subject matter of art. In reference to painting, she once said: "I do think in modern art that painters are specializing much too much in nightmares. I don't like nightmares, and I don't think nightmares sufficiently important to make a subject for art."[14]

In her biography of Isak Dinesen, Parmenia Migel recalls how during a stay in Paris, Isak Dinesen was invited to attend a performance of *The Diary of Anne Frank* and declined because of the painful wartime memories the play would evoke. "Her hosts," Miss Migel recounts, "graciously changed the tickets and she found herself instead at a dramatized version of *The Castle* by Frank Kafka. 'And that was a real night-

---

12. Ibid., p. 32.

13. *Shadows on the Grass,* pp. 107-108.

14. Curtis Cate, "Isak Dinesen," *Atlantic Monthly* (December 1959), p.151.

mare,' she said afterwards, 'worse even than Anne Frank's Diary.' "[15]

By assigning the dream an exalted position, Isak Dinesen is moving away from the interpretation of dreams as a means to a better understanding of the human personality and in the direction of dream as myth, as collective unconscious, and, therefore, as a basis for art and for the understanding of art. Jørgen Gustava Brandt points out that Isak Dinesen considers the dream more important than the dreamer.[16] Analysis, to her, is misleading man. According to her biographer, "she had a distinct aversion to Freudian probing as such, and as it manifested itself in modern literature." Miss Migel follows this comment with a hitherto unpublished fragment from one of Isak Dinesen's newspaper interviews with Bent Mohn in which Isak Dinesen (Tania) explains her position.

Mohn: You spoke of the unconscious. What do you think of Freud?

Tania: I don't really know enough about Freud to pronounce myself about him. I have always had beautiful, happy dreams myself, and have felt free and serene. I have never experienced what is called a nightmare, but my dreams have seldom had any real connection with my daily life. I believe that Freud did his time a great service by acknowledging "complexes" or facing up to them and thereby freeing people of much worry and anxiety. But I believe also that those who came after him frequently carried his searchings too far, or that they misunderstood them. The roots of a tree, a plant, may be deep down in soil or darkness; when we don't pull them up to examine or study them this does not mean that we are unaware of them or that we want to underestimate or deny them. We know very well that they are the life conditions of the tree, perhaps the most important part of it. There are in the nature and being of people many things, perhaps the most significant among them, that demand darkness and that need to go unobserved in order to grow soundly."[17]

---

15. *Titania* (New York, 1967), p. 273.
16. "Et Essay om Karen Blixen," *Heretica*, VI (1953), no. 2, p. 216.
17. *Titania*, p. 267.

She understands, says Brandt, that "the people of our time . . . have lost the roots and connections with superior powers."[18] It is the renewal of faith in the value of the dream, with its own truth, reality, and order, that will recover those roots and restore that connection with superior powers.

The difference beween the qualities of truth, reality, and order found in dream or art and those found in life are much like the difference between God and human beings as it occurs to Boris in "The Monkey" (SGT). "The real difference between God and human beings, he thought, was that God cannot stand continuance. No sooner has he created a season of a year, or a time of the day, than he wishes for something quite different, and sweeps it all away. No sooner was one a young man, and happy at that, than the nature of things would rush one into marriage, martyrdom or old age." God and the artist define truth in terms of change. Change of season, time of day, or fortune is the counterpart of the kind of change inherent in art—mask, dream, and disorder.[19] Such change is, on the highest level, the truth, reality, and order of the Logos.

Life, on the contrary, can only define truth, reality, and order in terms of earthly stability. While God loves change, thinks Boris, "human beings cleave to the existing state of things. All their lives they are striving to hold the moment fast, and are up against a *force majeure*." It is only natural, then, that human art will desire to subject itself to the laws of immutability and claim to find truth, reality, and order in permanence. "Their art itself," Boris realizes as he contemplates the art of human beings, "is nothing but the attempt to catch by all means the one particular moment, one mood, one light, the momentary beauty of one woman or one flower, and make it everlasting." God's art, and the art of those who are loyal to God's art, is, in contrast to human art, the art of continuance. In change only will it find its value; and its truth, reality, and order will be concealed within the mask, dream, and disorder

18. "Et Essay om Karen Blixen," p. 216.
19. I must of necessity use this term because there is no other way to indicate the different degree of order Isak Dinesen has in mind. Perhaps *unique order* might help.

that argue change. This means, apparently, that there can be no absolute truth, reality, or order in art except the absolute truth, reality, and order of change. Art that implies anything else, it seems, is false—or human—art.

This concept of the absolute value of change is an important affirmation of the value of an organic theory of art. If each separate work of art contains its own truth, reality, and order, then there is no external standard that can be brought to bear upon it other than the condition that the work of art conform to its own standards and not suggest that those particular standards are applicable to any other work of art. This is an assertion of the uniqueness of individual works of art, for duplication would be not only unnecessary but contradictory. This is why Isak Dinesen cannot talk about the specific nature of the mask, dream, or disorder that might appear in a work of art. All she can do is to insist that these elements be taken on their own terms, and that whenever they appear, they affirm the value of change.

If Isak Dinesen does, as I have attempted to show, favor an organic theory of art, she is to be excused for not being any more explicit than she is about the particulars of this theory on the grounds that no proponent of this theory has found it easy to explain. Because such a theory is based solely on the dictates of inner law, it is virtually impossible to make positive statements about it other than that it must obey inner law. As Oskar Walzel says in the conclusion of his book *German Romanticism:* "The theory of the organic work of art cannot be conveniently set to rule for the benefit of either poet or critic. . . . It is quite possible to deceive oneself."[20] We have seen Isak Dinesen caution the artist against such deception. The desire to follow the dictates of the true self can lead, says Walzel, to immorality and formlessness.[21] It is against this tendency that Isak Dinesen also warns her artist. She persists in favoring the organic theory, I think, because she sees in

---

20. (New York, 1965), pp. 290-291.
21. Ibid., p. 291.

anything conditioned by the inner law the same ethical quality that Schleiermacher, that great religious romantic, saw.[22]

Walzel insists that the organic theory can be defended— and was defended by German classicists as well as romanticists —in terms of landscape gardening and particularly the favorite symbol of the tree. A tree, as he explains it, grows according to its own inner law and is unlike any other tree. Its individual parts may be asymmetrical, but it achieves an organic unity as a whole tree which is peculiarly its own. Critics of the organic theory, who see it as a source of formlessness, can see in a tree, he says, the presence of form that is not externally imposed. A tree, he says, does not just grow to infinity, but develops within its own self-prescribed limits. So, too, he implies, does an organic work of art.[23]

If the organic theorist talks in what seem to be negative terms, it is owing, I think, to the fact that he can do little more than warn. He warns the artist what not to do, leaving what he must do to his own inner direction; and he warns the audience to expect a work of art to conform to externally imposed standards although he is unable to tell that audience very much about what to expect within any particular work of art. To use the symbol of the tree, one might say that Isak Dinesen is, in effect, cautioning the artist against pruning or grafting while she is justifying to the audience the presence of an asymmetrical branch or cluster of fruits. A work of art, like a tree, has its own truth, reality, and order.

---

22. Ibid., p. 290.
23. Ibid., pp. 291-293.

9

QUESTIONS OF TECHNIQUE
(Character, Distance, and Distortion)

IF HER FAITH in the absolute value of change makes it difficult for Isak Dinesen to be specific about questions of value, it makes it equally difficult for her to be specific about questions of technique. Questions of technique, like questions of value, must remain theoretical. She cannot prescribe the way in which a work of art is made, since each work makes its own demands and requires its own unique blend of rhetoric. There are, however, certain techniques or variations thereof that Isak Dinesen's ideal artist might be expected to use, out of fidelity to the Logos, even at the risk of incurring critical suspicion or disapproval.

Isak Dinesen's comments on technique, in short, are descriptive rather than prescriptive. She has, for example, nothing to say about the art of characterization, but she does have something to say about the subordination of character to plot. And when she is insisting that a character must feel secure in the hands of the author, she is not exhorting an author to save his characters; she is explaining what she feels is always the case in a good story, and why she thinks it is so. Similarly, her comments on distance and distortion are in the nature of apology rather than advice. Distancing and

79

distorting are not recommended devices; they are natural attributes.

It is in the area of character that Isak Dinesen is most explicit. In "The Heroine" (WT), the theology student Frederick Lamond compares the world to a big old book which falls open and slowly, on its own, turns one leaf after another. The book of the world is, of course, creation; and creation, as we have seen, is God's story—the divine manifestation of His Logos. In this story, this big old book of the world, the human characters, as Cardinal Salviati reminds the lady in black in "The Cardinal's First Tale" (LT), "do come forth on the sixth day only—by that time they were bound to come, for where the story is, the characters play an inferior role." Isak Dinesen carries this principle over into art, the function of which is to reflect the plot of creation.

Heroes, according to Isak Dinesen, exist by sole virtue of the greatness of the story. Whenever a character is elevated to a level superior to the story, he ceases to be a hero. "A story," says the cardinal, "has a hero to it, and you will see him clearly, luminous, and as upon a higher plane. Whatever he is in himself, the immortal story immortalizes its hero. Ali Baba, who in himself is nothing more than an honest woodcutter, is the adequate hero of a very great story." The novel, which Isak Dinesen finds an inferior art because of its emphasis on character at the expense of the story, is a threat to both story and characters. "By the time when the new literature shall reign supreme and you will have no more stories," says the cardinal, "you will have no more heroes. The world will have to do without them, sadly, until the hour when divine powers shall see fit, once more, to make a story for a hero to appear in."

It is clear, I think, that it is the salvation and not the subordination of character that is Isak Dinesen's first concern. She is not admonishing the artist to downgrade his characters, nor is she advising the critic to think that the highest art is that which sacrifices its characters to the gross appetites of action. What Isak Dinesen sees in the greatest art is that characters do not achieve heroic proportions except as they fulfill the demands of the plot. When the cardinal has finished explaining to the lady in black the way in which the story carries its characters along, the lady says: "What you call the divine art to me seems a hard and cruel game, which maltreats and mocks its human beings." "Hard and cruel it may seem," the cardinal replies, "yet we, who hold our high office as keepers and watchmen to the story, may tell you, verily, that to its human characters there is salvation in nothing else in the universe."

The cardinal then insists that the question of identity, which is the question closest to the human heart and the one to which mankind most insistently demands an answer, can only be answered within the framework of the story in which character defers to plot. "For within our whole universe," he says, "the story only has authority to answer that cry of heart of its characters, that one cry of heart of each of them: *'Who am I?'* "

As we have already seen in the discussion of the dangers of exceeding the limitations of art,[1] characters in Isak Dinesen's tales who attempt to exert their own will on the action, to step outside the story and alter its direction, become victims of their own machinations. What they suffer, above all, is a loss of identity, and this loss comes about by a process which begins when they assume a self-appointed role. The assumption of a self-appointed role leads them into the fatal error of complacency. And complacency deludes them into thinking that their role will never change. But the question of identity is bound up with the question of destiny, and destiny is a matter of becoming—of metamorphosis. The answer to the question: "Who am I?" can be found only within the greater context of the answer to the question: "What is my destiny?" And since the question of destiny is

---

1. Cf. Part II, chap. 1 (Masquerade and Reality).

answered only by the story itself—and the essence of the story is change—the character who asserts an identity without regard to change will reject his destiny and lose his identity.

It is the fact that characters lose rather than gain identity whenever they are exalted above the story that, I think, concerns Isak Dinesen. "The novel," says Robert Langbaum, in interpretation of Isak Dinesen's concept of characterization, "wants to look as though it was made by human beings, its characters. The events are the occasion for the characters to manifest themselves—which is why we do not want uncaused events, and why our sympathy for the characters exceeds anything called for by the events and may even at times contradict the events."[2] With the story the case is just the reverse, he explains. The story "wants to look as though it was made by God, or by the author who speaks with the voice of God in that he uses traditional plots, the meaning of which he as a person may not understand. The story is a manifestation of the divine order, and the characters are called into being to act out the story."[3]

Glenway Wescott in an essay on Isak Dinesen has this to say on the matter: "In the modern novel the most important thing is individuality; therefore it has to be, above all, explanatory and intimate. The question it asks as a rule is not *who* but what—what is he or she? what are you, the reader? or indeed, as it is often a subterfuge for autobiography, what am I? It is portraiture or self-portraiture, stepping from the frame only enough to demonstrate itself in action, or to teach a lesson, or to make a point. Whereas to the storyteller the events come first. Particularity of the personages involved comes second, as their activity depicts it, as destiny has brought it about."[4]

It is the idea of the manifestation of the divine order—

---

2. *The Gayety of Vision* (New York, 1965), p. 30.
3. Ibid.
4. "Isak Dinesen tells a tale," *Harper's Magazine*, CCXX, no. 1318 (March 1960), pp. 68-69.

destiny—and the place the characters assume in it that the
cardinal is trying to make clear to the lady in black in the
following explanation:

"A story, Madame, has a heroine—a young woman who by the
sole virtue of being so becomes the prize of the hero, and the
reward for his every exploit and every vicissitude. But by the
time when you have no more stories, your young women will be
the prize and reward of nobody and nothing. Indeed, I doubt
whether by then you will have any young women at all. For you
will not, then, see the wood for trees." Or, he added, as if in his
own thoughts, "it will be, at the best, a poor time, a sad time,
for a proud maiden, who will have no one to hold the stirrup to
her, but will have to come down from her milk-white steed to
trudge on a dusty road. And—alas! a poor and sad lover of hers
who will stand by to see his lady disrobed of her story or her epos
and, all naked, turned into an individual."

According to this passage, an individual must be, apparently, a person without a destiny and, therefore, without a
complete identity. Or, put another way, an individual is a
character in search of a story. "You will see the characters
of the true story clearly, as if luminous and on a higher
plane," says the cardinal, "and at the same time they may
look not quite human, and you may well be a little afraid of
them. That is all in the order of things." An individual is
human; a character is "not quite human" and will inspire
fear. This is so, it seems, because the individual is flat and
powerless and exposed, whereas the character has been
caught up in a role and has a sense of its power and is pro-
tected by the destiny he is fulfilling. The individual is in his
own hands and does not know which way to turn. The character is in the hands of the author, and his turnings are
prepared for him. This is the point Cardinal Salviati is trying
to make in the following passage:

"The story, according to its essence and plan, moves and places
these two young people, hero and heroine—together with their
confidants and competitors, friends, foes and fools—and goes on.
They need not distress themselves about material for the burnt

offering, for the story will provide. It will separate the two, in life, by the currents of the Hellespont and unite them, in death, in a Veronese tomb. It provides for the hero, and his young bride will exchange an old copper lamp for a new one, and the Chaldeans shall make out three bands and fall upon his camels and carry them away, and he himself with his own hand shall cook, for an evening meal with his mistress, the falcon which was to have saved the life of her small dying son. The story will provide for the heroine, and at the moment when she lifts up her lamp to behold the beauty of her sleeping lover it makes her spill one drop of burning oil on his shoulder. The story does not slacken its speed to occupy itself with the mien or bearing of its characters, but goes on. It makes the one faithful partisan of its old mad hero cry out in awe: 'Is this the promised end?'—goes on, and in a while calmly informs us: 'This is the promised end.' "

There is no promised end for individuals, for those "characters" who are superior to the story, because they have forfeited the security of destiny. Within the story, the characters do as they must, and by keeping the ideas of the author clear, they find their greatest happiness. Outside the story they have no guarantee (and neither has the reader) of the sort that Isak Dinesen thinks destiny affords. Councilor Mathiesen in the "The Poet" (SGT) steps outside the story, as we have seen, and thereby voluntarily rejects the security he would have found within the limitations of his own destiny. He might have come to an equally unpleasant end if he had submitted to his destiny, but he would have found consolation in accepting it as the will of a greater imagination than his own. In his dying moments, the councilor compares himself with King Lear and wonders why it was that the king "had somehow been so safe, so unshakenly secure," while he, the councilor, feels so abandoned. He then realizes that "the old King had been in the hands, whatever happened to him, of the great British poet, of William Shakespeare," and that "whatever he did, the author would see to it that things would somehow come out all right, that high and divine law and order would be maintained."

Again, this is not an admonition to the artist to do a particular thing, but an explanation to the critic of why he may find a certain thing done. The author who is keeping the ideas of the greater author clear will see to it that his own characters keep the ideas of their author clear. By maintaining "that high and divine law and order" of which the councilor speaks, the author will naturally subordinate his characters to the plot and thereby make them safe. In so doing, the author is behaving towards his characters in the same way that God behaves towards His. In submitting to destiny, man is secure in the knowledge that he is fulfilling the will of God. In submitting to plot, a character is secure in the knowledge that he is fulfilling the will of the author. A character is secure, that is, when his author allows him to fulfill his destiny. He is not secure, however, when his author is not himself aligned with his own destiny and is, therefore, incapable of embracing his characters in this one immense and inescapable context.

There is apparently no place in Isak Dinesen's view of art for the Promethean rebel, except perhaps as a subject for tragedy; and tragedy, as we shall see, is for her a human art, and therefore inferior to comedy, which is divine. Robert Langbaum's book *The Gayety of Vision* is based on the premise that Isak Dinesen's vision is essentially comic, and I think that much that has been said in this study up to this point will confirm that appraisal. The ultimate beauty of the dream, and the ultimate security of the story, are two of her most basic convictions; and both disallow the tragic vision. Tragedy demands that we identify very closely with the tragic figure so that we can share his emotions and experience a purgation of our own through him. Comedy requires a widening of the gulf between character and audience, and since Isak Dinesen exalts comedy, it is fitting that she should have something to say about the technique of distancing.

The subordination of character to plot is one step in the process of distancing, and, presumably, the security of the characters in the hands of the author is another. We neither pity characters in their misfortune, nor fear for ourselves in similar circumstances, when we know that they are working out their destinies and that this is right. What Aage Henriksen says about Isak Dinesen's own characters might well express her own concept of character distancing. "It is as if all the liquids have been pressed out of them, and they have been reduced to pure essence, but they have also taken on a certain ceramic glaze."[5] At this distance characters become allegorical, and the allegorical character is closer to an intellectual abstraction than to an emotional personality.

Langbaum has called the relationship between Mythos and Logos an intellectual dance.[6] It is the intellectual quality of art that interests Isak Dinesen, not the emotional. And this intellectual quality is best maintained through distancing. "Madame," says Cazotte to the grand duchess in "Ehrengard," "the Lord God, that great artist, at times paints his pictures in such a manner as to be best appreciated at a long distance. A hundred and fifty years hence your present predicament will have all the look of an idyll composed to delight its spectators. Your difficulty at this moment is that you are a little too close to it."

Cazotte recommends distancing as a way of adjusting to the distortion which, according to Isak Dinesen, has its natural place in art. Distortion, as a technique, serves two functions. On the one hand, it contributes to the effect of distancing by removing the audience even farther from that with which it would normally sympathize. On the other hand, it is a more accurate reflection of the kind of truth, reality, and order that art derives from the Logos and which, by virtue of the value of change, is so vastly different from the truth, reality, and order which humans impose. A dream is a distortion of reality, and to reflect it properly, the artist must also distort reality. In man's eyes creation itself is a distortion which he seems determined to organize and proportion. But the artist sees such distortion as only part of a

---

5. *Guder og galgefugle* (Oslo, 1956), p. 37.
6. *The Gayety of Vision*, p. 244.

greater harmony. He understands the principle of distortion and tries through it to reflect this greater harmony in his art.

The valet disguised as a cardinal in "The Deluge at Norderney" (SGT) is well aware of the vast difference between the "tremendous courage of the Creator of this world," who achieves harmony through distortion, and the cowardice of man, who cannot conceive of such distortion. "Every human being has, I believe, at times given room to the idea of creating a world himself," he says to Miss Nat-og-Dag, and then goes on to admit how feeble the human imagination would be if it were in possession of such a possibility. Only the artist, he says, might enjoy a share of this tremendous courage of the Creator. "What an overwhelming lesson to all artists!" he exclaims. "Be not afraid of absurdity; do not shrink from the fantastic. Within a dilemma, choose the most unheard-of, the most dangerous, solution. Be brave, be brave!"

When Count Augustus von Schimmelmann in "The Roads Round Pisa" (SGT) recalls his visit to the mirror room of the Panoptikon in Copenhagen, he is struck by "how much this was like real life." It is, of course, not at all like real life. He describes the room as a place "where you see yourself reflected, to the right and the left, in the ceiling and even on the floor, in a hundred glasses each of which distorts and perverts your face and figure in a different way—shortening, lengthening, broadening, compressing their shape, and still keeping some sort of likeness." Shortening, lengthening, broadening, and compressing are the hallmarks of distortion; yet the count can feel that this is like real life. Earlier he had claimed that "a glass tells you the truth about yourself," but now he is finding reality in a hall of distorted mirrors. The difference, it would seem, is that the truth about oneself, about the "individual," about the "character in search of a story," is found in an ordinary mirror. But it is not the truth about oneself that Isak Dinesen expects from art; it is the truth of destiny that is revealed through change. And change in art is reflected in the rearrangement of reality. By rearranging reality the mirror room suggests the masks and dreams and unique order that are a truer image of life than that which human timidity imposes upon it. Human art, the product of human timidity, is the ordinary mirror which tells the truth about the individual, and this is a source of passivity and melancholy. Divine art, the product of tremendous courage, is the hall of distorted mirrors which tells the truth about destiny, and this is a source of strength and joy.

Jonathan Swift held no ordinary mirror up to nature when he wrote *Gulliver's Travels*. The mirrors he used were the mirrors of the Panoptikon, in which the shapes of characters are shortened, lengthened, broadened, or compressed and still keep some sort of likeness. This is the point of "The Cardinal's Third Tale" (LT), in which Cardinal Salviati tells the story of Lady Flora, a woman who misunderstands Swift's use of distortion because she has been brought up to believe that Swift was ridiculing the size and not the behavior of men. Lady Flora happens to be a large person herself, and she hates Swift because during her childhood her father would always refer to the Brobdingnagians whenever he wanted to belittle her. As a result, she comes to think of all art as nothing more than a vicious exploitation of an unjust reality. In fact, she uses Swift as the means whereby she can "deride in toto the Almighty's work of creation."

With bitter irony she says to her confessor, Father Jacopo: "Look, Reverend Father, how little is needed, what slight transposition of dimensions suffices to reveal to us the true nature of your noble and beautiful universe." Father Jacopo attempts a rebuttal, but his argument, although it begins well and is essentially correct throughout, ends by offending Lady Flora. Father Jacopo argues that, rather than revealing the "true nature" of the universe, by which Lady Flora means the disgusting nature, a slight transposition of dimensions "will reveal to us with what subtle precision the harmony of our universe is adjusted and balanced." He goes on to explain that distortion "will tell us with what reverence we must eye the ordinance of the creator, so that not even in imagination do we presume to alter or transpose any jot or tittle thereof." This much of his explanation is sound and inoffensive because it is beautifully vague. But then he says: "The shortening or lengthening of a single string of an instrument may enable us to distort, aye, to annihilate its music. But surely, surely the fact does not justify us in blaming that master who built the violin."

Lady Flora might have been able to accept, after all, a natural distortion if it would reveal with what subtle precision the harmony of our universe is adjusted and balanced. But the analogy of the string of an instrument, which, when shortened or lengthened, annihilates its music, implies tampering on the part of the player; and since she does not distinguish, apparently, between player and builder, she finds this sufficient reason to continue to believe that she has been unjustly treated and that art is ridicule.

What Father Jacopo should have made clear, and what the cardinal implies in his telling of the story, is that distortions in art function not to direct our attention to the distortion itself but to something beyond it that we might never have noticed had proportion been respected. She fails to see, and Father Jacopo is unable to make her see, that the giants in Swift are not ridiculous for their size but for their actions. The cardinal suggests that Lady Flora has so confused life and art that she thinks of herself as a character in *Gulliver's Travels* rather than in life, and she is suffering because she is in a story but she does not enjoy the protection of the storyteller.

It may be concluded, I think, that the questions of value and technique discussed in these chapters will not suffice to give us a practical way to evaluate form in a work of art. In a sense, they are negative considerations that tell us what not to look for. We must *not* demand routine concepts of truth, reality, and order. We must *not* demand highly developed characterization, a sense of involvement, or accuracy of proportion.

Isak Dinesen does not say, of course, that these properties cannot exist in a work of art; she simply suggests that their absence must not prevent one from discovering the presence of possibly more important things. Again she is being defensive, and with cause. Her own writing was such a radical departure from the social realism of the day that she worried lest readers would be too quick to dismiss her tales as curiosities. But she does not claim a unique position. If anything, her plea for understanding is a plea for the universal and eternal values of art. If she betrays a fear of anything, it is of those who will impose external standards on art and find it wanting; and the matters that have been under discussion here are, above all, reminders that each work of art must be judged on its own merit.

10

TRAGEDY AND COMEDY

ISAK DINESEN makes a distinction between tragedy and comedy which is similar to the one she makes between the novel and the story. Tragedy, like the novel, is a human art; comedy, like the story, is a divine one. "It may be, then," says Adam in "Sorrow-Acre" (SGT), "that we hold tragedy to be, in the scheme of life, a noble, a divine phenomenon." His uncle is quick to correct him. "Aye, a noble phenomenon, the noblest on earth," he says. "But of the earth only, and never divine. Tragedy is the privilege of man, his highest privilege. . . . The true art of the gods is the comic."

According to this distinction, tragedy cannot be an earthly reflection of the divine creative force unless it is considered as a part of comedy—much as Isak Dinesen considers nightmare as an incomplete dream. Northrop Frye has said that we reconcile ourselves to tragedy because it leads by implication to comedy. This implication Isak Dinesen would call the comic vision, I think; and I think she would insist that it be present before a work with tragic elements could truly be labeled the highest form of art. If Frye is right, says Robert Langbaum in his appraisal of Isak Dinesen's vision, then tragicomedy would be the vehicle of this complete or ultimate

vision.[1] Langbaum points out, in defense of Isak Dinesen's in-
clination towards tragicomedy, that the Greeks finished with
the tragicomedies of Euripides and that Shakespeare wrote
tragicomedies towards the end of his career. From such evidence as this, Langbaum concludes that the comic vision which
Isak Dinesen favors arises out of the completion of the tragic
knowledge.[2]

If we are to define tragedy, then, as Isak Dinesen conceives of it, we must approach it by way of an understanding
of tragic knowledge. Once we know what that is, we will be
able to understand why she assigns certain properties to tragedy
and how she relates these properties to the limited view of
tragedy as a human art and to the expanded view of tragedy
as a part of the comic vision.

"Tragedy," says the old artist in "Copenhagen Season"
(LT), "far from being the outcome of the fall of man is on
the contrary the counter-measure taken by man against the
sordid and dull conditions brought upon him by his fall." To
begin with, then, we know that tragic knowledge is a knowledge of the sordid and dull conditions of life after the loss of
Eden. In the next sentence, the artist says that man was "flung
from heavenly glory and enjoyment into necessity and routine."
Necessity and routine, then, must be among the sordid and dull
conditions against which man rebels through tragedy.

I think it can also be said that these conditions are a
part of as well as a reason for tragedy. The dull and sordid
conditions of Anne-Marie's life as detailed in "Sorrow-Acre"
precipitate her tragedy, and they include the necessity of
sacrificing herself to save her son's life. She is a widow with a
bad reputation, and her son is of questionable character. Her
sacrifice is as much a reaction against the miserable circumstances of her life as it is the result of them. Her tragedy, however, is but a part of the greater comedy that frames "Sorrow-
Acre." Isak Dinesen wrote the story in reaction to the traditional legend of Anne-Marie as a Christ figure. Isak Dinesen's

---

1. *The Gayety of Vision* (New York, 1965), p. 55.
2. Ibid.

retelling is a deliberate attempt to place the tragedy of Anne-Marie within the cosmic perspective of manorial culture.[3]

I think Isak Dinesen would say that tragic knowledge is the same as the knowledge of evil, which is half of the knowledge man acquired through his disobedience in the garden. Knowledge of dull and sordid conditions is knowledge of evil, and it requires knowledge of good before the comparison can be made. Knowledge of good, then, would be comic knowledge, or the knowledge of the gods.[4] The knowledge of necessity, for instance, is evil knowledge since it is unknown to the gods. "Tragedy," says the old lord, is subject "to the dire laws of necessity. . . . But the gods, whom we must believe to be unacquainted with and incomprehensive of necessity, can have no knowledge of the tragic."

Another part of tragic knowledge is the knowledge of shame from which honor is born. Honor, as Isak Dinesen means it, is the wish on the part of man to regain his dignity before God.[5] "In Paradise there was no idea of honor," says the old artist. Honor arose out of shame ("And they saw that they were naked") which fostered remorse, or guilt. "All tragedies," says the old artist, "are determined by the idea of honor. The idea of honor does not save humanity from suffering, but it enables it to write a tragedy." Although tragedy does not save humanity from suffering, the old artist does admit that man believes "it is salvation and beatification."

Tragedy, then, can be defined, according to what Isak Dinesen has said, as a human phenomenon in which man, out of a sense of honor, rebels against the conditions brought about by the Fall by contrasting them with the Edenic ideal in an attempt to regain his innocence. Or she might prefer

---

3. Ibid., p. 32.
4. Knowledge of good—or comic knowledge—absorbs and transforms knowledge of evil—or tragic knowledge—just as dream absorbs and transforms nightmare. The reverse, however, is not true. Tragic knowledge does not contain comic knowledge; it is incomplete comic knowledge.
5. Cf. Part II, chap. 4 (The Measure of Distress).

to say, simply, that tragedy is the imitation of lost destiny. Man cannot regain this lost destiny, as Isak Dinesen sees it, through tragedy alone, however. The ultimate purpose of all art is to reflect cosmic intent, and the ultimate effect is to regain naiveté through submission to destiny. Neither this purpose nor this effect can be achieved except through the comic vision.

Tragedy, in Isak Dinesen's hands, is a protean concept. Any way of approaching it veers towards the comic. In their discussion of her concept of tragedy, Hanne Marie and Werner Svendsen are also troubled by this elusiveness. According to Isak Dinesen, they say: "Everything here in the world must be dearly paid for"—a tragic view—"but it is worth it to pay the high price"[6]—a comic view. And when they say that for Isak Dinesen, "life's highest meaning is concealed in tragedy,"[7] they imply that its highest meaning might very well be revealed in comedy. Concealment, in other words, is only half the picture.

I think that Isak Dinesen's one truly tragic figure is Councilor Mathiesen in "The Poet" (SGT), and it is to him that we can look for some illumination on the question of tragic flaw. His idyllic life is interrupted by the knowledge that he can never be the poet he has always dreamed of being. The necessity of being something else he finds tiresome, and as a countermeasure against this dull condition, he undertakes to arrange the lives of others in accordance with a plan which will afford him a vicarious success as a poet. This decision to meddle in his own destiny—and the destiny of others—to appoint himself as the best judge of what should be, is, I think, his fatal mistake. We have seen this mistake in operation before, and on the basis of Isak Dinesen's insistent comment on the subject, I would suggest that a tragic hero commits his tragic error at the moment when he takes destiny into his own hands. What is a countermeasure against the sordid and dull conditions brought about by the Fall if

---

6. *Geschichte der danischen Literatur* (Copenhagen, 1964), p. 479.
7. Ibid.

not a dangerous presumption? The dull and sordid conditions will remain—or get worse—as the presumption works its way, by dire necessity, to its grim conclusion.

It is in keeping with Isak Dinesen's general philosophy, I believe, to say that those who willingly submit to their destinies are comic figures and those who do not are tragic figures. Such a definition does not afford tragic figures the exalted station that Aristotle assigns them. Isak Dinesen's tragic hero is more pitiful than pitiable. For one thing, she excludes the nobility from the role of tragic hero; and for another, she specifies no moral qualifications. "Here on earth," says the old lord in "Sorrow-Acre," "we, who stand in lieu of the gods and have emancipated ourselves from the tyranny of necessity, should leave to our vassals their monopoly of tragedy, and for ourselves accept the comic with grace." Pity, for Isak Dinesen, is a degrading emotion, not to be directed, it would seem, towards God or His mouthpieces. "In pitying, or condoling with your god," says the old lord, "you deny and annihilate him, and such is the most horrible of atheisms." Moreover, the effect of an action differs between those who stand in lieu of the gods and their vassals. "Indeed," says the old lord, "the very same fatality, which, in striking the burgher or peasant, will become tragedy, with the aristocrat is exalted to the comic."

The old lord explains this difference in effect according to the rule of necessity which, as we have already seen, does not apply to the gods, or, by implication, to their lieutenants. "When they are brought face to face with it," he says, "they will, according to my experience, have the good taste and decorum to keep still, and not interfere." He demonstrates this principle by not interfering in the necessity that is driving Anne-Marie to her death in the rye field. In reply to his nephew's uneasiness over Anne-Marie's suffering, the old lord says: "Only a boorish and cruel master—a parvenu, in fact—will make a jest of his servants' necessity, or force the comic upon them. Only a timid and pedantic ruler, a *petit-maître,* will fear the ludicrous on his own behalf." It is the old

lord's own situation that is ludicrous, of course. Anne-Marie's
son will live, whereas his own son and only heir has already
died; and Adam is destined to take over the line and per-
petuate it by cuckolding his uncle. After Anne-Marie has
come to her tragic end, the old lord reappears to restore the
comic vision. At the end of the story we see him, a silly,
overdressed little man, "stepping along a little, and again
standing still" on the rye field that the old woman's suffering
has immortalized.

Anne-Marie's choice, which we have every reason to believe is the wrong one, is made tragic by the dignity it gives her
in contrast to the sadly funny figure the old lord cuts. Her ideal
is permanence, and she destroys herself in an effort to keep
things as they are, in spite of—or maybe because of—the fact
that her own life has been subject to some bitter changes (a
dead husband, a murdered child). The old lord, faced with
the necessity of change in his dynasty, has the good taste and
decorum to keep still, and not interfere. There is the sug-
gestion, in Isak Dinesen's concept of tragedy, of self-punishment—the heaping upon oneself of punishment in excess of
what one deserves, or receives. This self-punishment is a result
of the shame man feels over his fallen state and an expression
of his desire to atone, which his honor compels him towards at
his own expense.

If tragedy is not the art of the gods, it is at least the
highest art of man, in Isak Dinesen's estimate. Expelled from
Eden, says the old artist in "Copenhagen Season" (LT), "in
one supreme effort of his humanity he created tragedy. How
pleasantly surprised was not then the Lord. 'This creature,'
He exclaimed, 'was indeed worthy of being created. I have
done well in making him, for he can make things for me which
without him I cannot make.' "

"Tragedy," the old lord in "Sorrow-Acre" explains, "is
the privilege of man, his highest privilege. The God of the
Christian Church Himself, when He wished to experience
tragedy, had to assume human form. And even at that . . . the
tragedy was not wholly valid, as it would have become had the

hero of it been, in very truth, a man. The divinity of Christ conveyed to it a divine note, the moment of comedy. The real tragic part, by the nature of things, fell to the executors, not to the victim." The executors, of course, were trying to oppose tragic knowledge with bourgeois virtues. By crucifying Christ, they made a futile attack against change—for Christ is, to Isak Dinesen, the arch symbol of metamorphosis—and thus suffered the tragic end they had planned for their victim.

It is understandably to the comic, then, that Isak Dinesen pays the highest tribute. "The true art of the gods is the comic," says the old lord. "The comic is a condescension of the divine to the world of man; it is the sublime vision, which cannot be studied, but must ever be celestially granted. In the comic the gods see their own being reflected as in a mirror, and while the tragic poet is bound by strict laws, they will allow the comic artist a freedom as unlimited as their own." The strict laws of tragedy include the tragic knowledge of the conditions of the fallen state, necessity, and honor; and the bourgeois virtues of complacency, permanence, and self-appointment. The mirror in which the comic artist reflects the gods is the mirror of the Mythos reflecting the Logos. For this art there is no law other than loyalty to the Logos, or, as Isak Dinesen once defined humor, a "strange kind of reliance on the grace of God."[8]

If one can define Isak Dinesen's concept of comedy, it would have to be thus: Comedy is a divine phenomenon (Logos) reflected in human terms (Mythos) out of a sense of loyalty, in which the conditions brought about by the Fall are accepted with a rapture which culminates in a reconciliation of all opposites (blank page). Or, as she might prefer it: Comedy is the imitation of the willing submission to destiny. We shall see in the ensuing section how the blank page becomes the ultimate comic vision which is total reconciliation through submission to destiny.

---

8. "Breve fra et Land i Krig" *Dansk Shrivekunst,* ed. Erling Nielsen (Oslo, 1955), p. 20.

IV

THE BLANK PAGE

11

EXPLICATION OF "THE BLANK PAGE"

THE PART WHICH Isak Dinesen assigns to the audience in the realization of a work of art is as demanding as that which she assigns the artist. It is not surprising, then, that the listeners in Isak Dinesen's tales are usually storytellers themselves, for to participate fully in a story, a listener must be able to involve himself in it as deeply as the teller, to assist the teller, as it were, in the creation of the story—just as man assists God in the creation of the world. The point at which the interdependent roles of author and audience merge is that point beyond the work of art which Isak Dinesen calls the *blank page*. It is at this point that the story which has been properly told will unfold its deeper meaning in the mind of the audience—will, in the silence that speaks, bring about the reconciliation of opposites which is the highest effect of art.

The effect of art, which the blank page symbolizes, is similar to the effect produced by the music of Adrian Leverkühn in Thomas Mann's *Doctor Faustus*. Leverkühn, because of his pact with Mephistopheles—a pact which Thomas Mann suggests is the price of the artist's humanity—is unable to write music which will convey within its own form the effect he desires. The element of compassion is missing from his music (as it is, interestingly enough, from many of Isak Dinesen's tales), but it is this element which he finally manages to suggest by concluding a musical composition at that point at which the note of compassion is implicit in the soundless moment that follows. This soundless moment is Isak Dinesen's blank page.

A close look at the tale "The Blank Page" (LT) will reveal, I think, what Isak Dinesen means by this term and how she arrives at it. The tale is a simple one and is told before an ancient city gate by "an old coffee-brown, black-veiled woman who made her living by telling stories." She is an illiterate old woman who has been educated in the art of storytelling by her grandmother. "With my grandmother," says the old woman, "I went through a hard school. 'Be loyal to the story,' the old hag would say to me. 'Be eternally and unswervingly loyal to the story.' 'Why must I be that, Grandmother?' I asked her. 'Am I to furnish you with reasons, baggage?' she cried. 'And you mean to be a story-teller! Why, you are to become a story-teller, and I shall give you my reasons!' " The grandmother proceeds to give her reasons, but her explanation does not make the idea of loyalty to the story any clearer to her granddaughter because it is rendered in terms of the blank page. " 'Where the story-teller is loyal, eternally and unswervingly loyal to the story, there, in the end, silence will speak. Where the story has been betrayed, silence is but emptiness. But we, the faithful, when we have spoken our last word, will hear the voice of silence. Whether a small snotty lass understands it or not.' "

The old woman knows that this explanation is as enigmatic to her present audience as it was to herself at the time she first heard it. It is only a lifetime (over two hundred years, she says!) of storytelling that has made the reasons clear to her. She expresses, however, some hesitation about imparting her secret; but she is, as we have seen Isak Dinesen herself be, as eager to assist her audience in understanding her art as she is reluctant to give herself away. "We," she says at last, "the old women who tell stories, we know the story of the blank page. But we are somewhat averse to telling it, for it might well, among the uninitiated, weaken our own credit. All the same, I am going to make an exception with you, my sweet and pretty lady and gentleman of the generous hearts. I shall tell it to you."

In her own defense, therefore, but at her own risk, the old woman tells the story of "The Blank Page." It is of interest to note that her audience consists of the smallest possible number and arrangement of persons—one man and one woman—for the proper understanding of the tale; for it is a story of the reconciliation of opposites, of which man and woman are one example. The only demand the old woman makes upon her audience is that it be of a generous heart.

The tale of "The Blank Page" is about an order of Carmelite sisters who live in a convent high up in the mountains of Portugal and who grow flax and make linen for royal bridal beds. They have been performing this singular service since the days of the Crusades, and although their convent is crumbling and their order declining, they continue to perform it right up until the time the story is being told. The bridal sheets are used for the wedding night only. The next morning the stained sheet is displayed from the balcony of the palace to attest to the virginity of the royal bride. Then, the stained portion is cut out and returned, with great ceremony, to the convent where it is encased in a gold frame bearing the name and royal crest, and hung in a gallery with many others like it.

Among this gallery of marked linen squares, there is, however, one square of unstained linen whose gold frame bears a royal crest but no name. "The linen within the frame," says the old woman, "is snow-white from corner to corner, a blank page. . . . It is in front of this piece of pure, white linen that the old princesses of Portugal—worldly wise, dutiful, long-suffering queens, wives and mothers—and their noble old playmates, bridesmaids, and maids-of-honor have most often stood still." The old woman concludes her tale with this statement: "It is in front of the blank page that old and young nuns, with the Mother Abbess herself, sink into deepest thought."

On the simplest level, the unstained square of linen suggests several possible meanings. Whereas the stained square means merely that the bride was a virgin at the time of her wedding and that the marriage was consummated during the wedding night, the snow-white square could mean that the bride was not a virgin, that someone had claimed *jus primae noctis,* that the marriage was not consummated, even that the bride had been visited by a god. The important thing to the old storyteller is that the unstained piece of linen was installed in the gallery because of a tradition of loyalty in the royal blood that could not allow leaving it out.

The seed for the flax which the sisters grow does not come from the area around the convent, we are told early in the story, but from the Holy Land. "Thus does the linen of the Convento Velho draw its true virtue from the fact that the very first linseed was brought home from the Holy Land itself by a Crusader." This is the first virtue, the storyteller explains, because "the very first germ of a story will come from some mystical place outside the story itself." This linseed, the germ that comes from some mystical place outside the story itself, is the Logos which the Carmelite sisters turn into Mythos by growing flax, weaving linen, and producing bridal sheets on which many royal destinies are reflected in patterns of blood.

The stained squares from these bridal sheets that hang in the gallery of the convent testify to the human story of the fall of man and his subsequent suffering. Each square is a tragedy, a symbol of man's shame which his sense of honor has ennobled through ceremony and display. Yet the mysterious seed of life is transmitted by means of this tragedy, and the spinster playmates of the brides gaze upon these squares of stained linen "sighing a little and smiling a little," aware, no doubt, of their own exemption from, yet oblique involvement in, this tragic reminder. These old virgins read meanings into the shapes of the stains and "remember how once, from the markings on the canvas, omens were drawn."

As these old ladies "compare the fulfillment to the omen," they are judging how truly the markings on the canvas have foretold the destinies of the royal brides they once knew and

served. They take stock of "happy events and disappointments
—coronations and jubilees, court intrigues and wars, the birth
of heirs to the throne, the alliances of younger generations
of princes and princesses, the rise or decline of dynasties." In
returning their Mythos unto God, the sisters of the convent,
like artists, have marked their canvases with the blood of
reality which they, as arbiters, have transformed by turning
what are merely stained sheets into masks that contain within
them the truth of destiny and change. "Within the faded markings of the canvases people of some imagination and sensibility may read all the signs of the Zodiac: the Scales, the
Scorpion, the Lion, the Twins. Or they may there find pictures
from their own world of ideas: a rose, a heart, a sword—or
even a heart pierced through with a sword."

Each square is a work of art, each is unique, and each
must be judged separately according to its own rules and
meaning. "Each separate canvas with its coroneted name-
plate," says the old storyteller, "has a story to tell, and each has
been set up in loyalty to the story." It is in their loyalty to the
story, of course, that they are united—and in their relationship
to the one unstained square, which is the other half of their
story. For it is the one snow-white square that robs the gallery
of its tragedy by turning the whole scene towards the comic.

The old spinsters "compare the fulfillment of the omen,
sighing a little and smiling a little." The sigh and the smile
suggest an equal division between the success and the failure
of the omen to be fulfilled. And since the sigh and smile are
expressed before the same canvas, it must be true that no
canvas represents a true fusion of omen and destiny, or, in the
terms we have been using, Logos and Mythos. The one canvas
that is an exception to this conclusion is the one that is unstained, "snow-white from corner to corner, a blank page."
As Logos, the canvas was handed down unstained; and as
Mythos, it is returned unstained. We know that it has been on
a bridal bed; otherwise, "the royal papa and mamma" would
not have "ordered this canvas to be framed and hung up."

"The story-tellers themselves before it draw their veils

over their faces and are dumb." In front of it, the "old and young nuns, with the Mother Abbess, sink into deepest thought." In two deft strokes, Isak Dinesen puts the artist and the priest aside to focus attention on the aristocratic bride. Which bride is it before whose square of wedding sheet the storytellers grow dumb and nuns sink into deepest thought? Or is there, indeed, a bride at all?

The effect of the blank page might be thought of as an overpowering awareness of the possibilities of the Logos. The varieties of stains on the other squares are only ways of suggesting the infinite varieties that might be marked upon the squares. But the blank page suggests, at once, all stains and no stains. No Mythos can reflect the infinite possibilities of the Logos. The most the Mythos can do is to call attention to something beyond itself; and it is this something that Isak Dinesen means, I think, by the blank page. This is why she makes the artist subservient to the tale and the tale subservient to the effect. The line from Logos to Mythos must, as long as man is mortal, pass through the artist and his art. But the ultimate effect of what the artist does through his art must be to reconcile Mythos and Logos to the exclusion of everything else.

In the presence of the blank page, all those who stand in lieu of God, all God's mouthpieces, retreat. The storyteller is dumb, the mother abbess pensive, and the royal bride whose snow-white canvas overwhelms them is nameless. Art, like church and castle, is irrelevant in heaven.

12

LOCKED CASKETS

"All human relationships have in them something monstrous and cruel," says Charlie Despard in "A Consolatory Tale" (WT). "But the relation of the artist to the public is amongst the most monstrous. Yes, it is as terrible as marriage." Isak Dinesen is fond of using the analogy of a love affair in talking about the artist and his public because she finds in a love affair the best expression of a willingness to accept absurdity and enigma and to do so passionately.

Matteo, one of the old men in "Tales of Two Old Gentlemen" (LT), quotes his grandfather on the subject of the love affair as the best description of the relationship between God and man. He feels that women understand this relationship better because " 'Man, troubled and perplexed about the relation between divinity and humanity, is ever striving to find a foothold in the matter by drawing on his own normal experience. He will view it in the light of relations between tutor and pupil, or of commander and soldier, and he will lose breath—and heart—in search and investigation.' " The mundane relationships which Matteo's grandfather mentions need not prevent us, however, from exempting the artist-public relationships from that list and comparing it with the cosmic love affair which, he says, is the way women view the relationship

between divinity and humanity. We have already seen how
Isak Dinesen compares the artist to God, and we shall see the
extent to which her comments on the relation of the artist to
the public affirm the cosmic analogy. "The ladies, whose
nature is nearer to the nature of the deity," says Matteo's
grandfather, ". . . see the relation between the Cosmos and
the Creator quite plainly as a love affair. And in a love affair
search and investigation is an absurdity, and unseemly."

That Isak Dinesen wants us to see the relation of the
artist to the public in the same way that the ladies see the
relation between the cosmos and the Creator is made clear in
the following passage from "The Dreaming Child" (WT). In
this passage the author is discussing the relationship between
Mamzell Ane, an old storyteller, and the child Jens, who, as a
God-like child, has a touch of the poet.

The idea of this majestic, radiant world, in the mind of little
Jens merged with that of his own inexplicable isolation in life
into a great dream, or fantasy. He was so lonely in Madame
Mahler's house because one of the houses of Mamzell Ane's tales
was his real home. In the long days, when Madame Mahler stood
by her wash-tub, or brought her washing out into town, he
fondled, and played with, the picture of this house and of the
people who lived in it, and who loved him so dearly. Mamzell Ane,
on her side, noted the effect of her *épopée* on the child, realized
that she had at last found the ideal audience, and was further
inspired by the discovery. The relation between the two developed
into a kind of love-affair; for their happiness, for their very
existence they had become dependent upon each other.

Charlie Despard in "A Consolatory Tale" spells out the
nature of this dependence and its implications.

"We are, each of us, awaiting the consent, or the co-operation
of the other to be brought into existence at all. Where there is
no work of art to look at, or to listen to, there can be no public
either; that is clear, I suppose, even to you? And as to the work
of art, now—does a painting exist at which no one looks?—does a
book exist which is never read? No, Aeneas, they have got to be
looked at; they have got to be read. And again by the very act of
being looked at, or of being read, they bring into existence that
formidable being, the spectator, the which, sufficiently multiplied

—and we want it multiplied, miserable creatures that we are—will become the public. And so there we are, as you see, at the mercy of it."

The public, of course, is equally at the mercy of the artist. It may embrace the artist in a dance, but it is the partner that follows, not leads; and, as such, one of its obligations is to be content with understanding only half of what the artist is saying and to believe that the half is greater than the whole. It has already been noted that Mira Jama makes this point in "The Dreamers" (SGT), and the point is made again in "The Poet" (SGT) by Count Augustus von Schimmelmann, the poet turned critic. "Beware of the delights of fairyland," he says. "To poor mortals the value of pleasure, surely, lies in its rarity. Did not the sages of old tell us: He is a fool who knows not the half to be more than the whole? Where pleasure goes on forever, we run the risk of becoming blasé, or, according to our young friend [Anders Kube, the real poet] of dying." This is the kind of joyful surrender, of course, that is more likely in a love affair than in any less emotional relationship. Lovers savor the enigmatic.

It is interesting to note that while the relationship between artist and public, as Isak Dinesen sees it, is best described in emotional terms, the effect of art on the audience is, as we shall see, largely an intellectual (and ultimately a spiritual) one. This is a decidedly modern refinement of the purpose of the tale, which has been traditionally more visceral than cerebral. "People love to be frightened," says Mira Jama, in "The Dreamers" as he recalls the old days. "The great princes, fed up with the sweets of life, wished to have their blood stirred again. The honest ladies, to whom nothing ever happened, longed to tremble in their beds just for once. The dancers were inspired to a lighter pace by tales of flight and pursuit. Ah, how the world loved me in those days!"

Emotion is not lacking, of course, in Isak Dinesen's concept of the effect of art upon the audience. The kinds of emotions which Mira Jama refers to may no longer be desirable for their own sake, but they have been subsumed by the

intellectuality and distilled as spirituality—if we think of
spirituality as that point at which emotion and intellect meet.
At this level the stirred blood and the trembling become contrition and pride, and it is in this sort of response that the work
of art is verified. Charlie Despard in "A Consolatory Tale" is
very much concerned with the problem of the audience, and he
is acutely aware of the necessity of evoking the right response
from it. He explains this to Aeneas Snell in a passage that is
Isak Dinesen's most graphic explication of the artist's fearful
relationship with his public.

"All works of art are beautiful and perfect. And all of them are,
at the same time, hideous, ludicrous, complete failures. At the
moment when I begin a book it is always lovely. I look at it, and
I see that it is good. While I am at the first chapter of it it is so
well balanced, there is such sweet agreement between the various
parts, as to make its entirety a marvellous harmony and generally,
at that time, the last chapter of the book is the finest of all. But
it is also, from the very moment it is begun, followed by a horrible
shadow, a loathsome, sickening deformity, which all the same is
like it, so that I myself will not recognize my work, but will shrink
from it, like the farm wife from the changeling in her cradle, and
cross myself at the idea that I have ever held it to be my own
flesh and bone. Yes, in short and in truth, every work of art is
both the idealization and the perversion, the caricature of itself.
And the public has power to make it, for good or evil, the one
or the other. When the heart of the public is moved and shaken
by it, so that with tears of contrition and pride they acclaim it as
a masterpiece, it becomes that masterpiece which I did myself at
first see. And when they denounce it as insipid and worthless,
it becomes worthless. But when they will not look at it at all—
voilà, as they say in this town, it does not exist. In vain shall I cry
to them: 'Do you see nothing there?' They will answer me, quite
correctly: 'Nothing at all, yet all that is I see.' Aeneas, if the
case of the artist be so with his public, it is not good to paint or
to write books."

The spiritual effect—contrition and pride—is the reconciliation of emotion and intellect, and is arrived at, not at the
point of understanding within the work of art ("all that is I
see"), but at a point beyond the work of art, toward which the
work of art points, where artist and audience, like Mythos and

Logos, meet—at the blank page. It is interesting to note, I think, how the state of contrition and pride in which the ideal audience finds itself parallels the state of humility and pride in which the ideal artist finds himself when he is in touch with divine inspiration.

Despard then goes on to discuss the relationship between artist and audience in terms of the Job story. In his dialogue with God in "The Young Man with the Carnation," the tale that opens *Winter's Tales,* Despard had assumed the role of Job. Now, in "A Consolatory Tale," the final tale in the book, Despard says that he sees himself in the place of the Lord. The explanation for the fact that *Winter's Tales* begins with Despard in the role of Job and ends with him in the role of the Lord lies in an understanding of what Isak Dinesen sees as a pattern in the lines of communication between God, artist, and public. God's position at the top is always superior to that of the artist or the public. The public's position at the bottom is always inferior to that of God or the artist. But the artist is in a unique position; his position is inferior to God's but superior to the public's. Therefore, in communication with God, the artist is Job, and he receives the same sort of treatment from God that he, himself, dispenses to the public.

The artist must be as merciless with the public as God is with him. When Aeneas Snell calls for a show of mercy on the part of the artist toward his public, Despard says: "Mercy? What are you talking about? . . . We cannot show mercy to one another. The public cannot be merciful to an artist; if it were merciful it would not be the public. Thank God for that, in any case. Neither can an artist be merciful to his public, or it has, at least, never been tried." There can be, then, no compromises. The artist can make no concessions to the artist. Only by adhering faithfully to the demands of their separate but interdependent roles can they, together, agree upon what constitutes a work of art. The way is not always easy, Isak Dinesen seems to warn, but the rewards are great, and anything less than merciless cooperation is, apparently, a fraud and a deceit.

Something of the tension and the struggle is suggested by Despard as he further explains the Job analogy. "I have behaved to my reader as the Lord behaves to Job," he says. "I know, none so well, none so well as I, how the Lord needs Job as a public, and cannot do without him." We have seen earlier how God needed a critical eye in the Garden and how he praised man for inventing tragedy. Now Isak Dinesen affirms the role of man as audience and makes this role a rather exalted one. "Yes," Despard continues, "it is even doubtful whether the Lord be not more dependent upon Job than Job upon the Lord." He then abruptly applies this idea to his own relationship with his reader. "I have laid a wager with Satan about the soul of my reader," he says. "I have marred his path and turned terrors upon him, caused him to ride on the wind and dissolved his substance, and when he waited for light there was darkness. And Job does not want to be the Lord's public any more than my public wishes to be so to me."

From the time when, as a young girl, she plagued her sister with stories every evening as they brushed each other's hair, until the day when, as an old woman, she entertained millions on television in the United States and Denmark, Isak Dinesen never lost her respect for the audience—and never did she condescend to be easy on it. What she sought, and what she urges the artist to seek, is not the transient approbation of the public, but its loyal opposition. The opposition of the audience is, in a sense, the intellectual, or critical, half of its response—that half which demands relentlessly that the artist remain true to the story and drive it to its utmost consequences. The loyalty of the audience is expressed in its faith in the possibilities and wisdom of art. In what the author calls "words of wisdom," the poet-turned-critic Count Augustus von Schimmelmann in "The Poet" explains to Councilor Mathiesen this concept in terms of religion—but the concept applies equally well to art.

"When . . . you and I, on our morning walk, pass a pawnbroker's shop, and, pointing at a painted board in the window, on which is written 'Clothes mangled here,' you say to me: 'Look, clothes are mangled here—I shall go and bring my washing,' I smile at you, and inform you that you will find neither mangle nor mangler here, that the painted board is for sale.

"Most religions are like the board, and we smile at them.

"But I should have no opportunity of smiling, or of feeling or showing my superiority, and, in fact, the painted board would not be there at all, if, at some time or other, some people had not believed in the possibility, in the wisdom, of mangling clothes, had not even been firmly convinced of the existence of their own mangle, with which clothes were indeed mangled."

The artist needs trust, says Jørgen Gustava Brandt in his essay on Isak Dinesen. "He must find almost unlimited trust from his audience if his work of art is to come about."[1] The sign in the window would not be there, art would not exist, it seems, if the public did not believe in the possibility and wisdom of art and was not firmly convinced of its own ability to respond. Brandt points out that Isak Dinesen does not deal in artificial language and contrived symbols. He maintains what she herself has confirmed, that her signs mean what they say, just as, apparently, the painted board in the window means what it says. It affirms the existence of a possibility which it did not originate. It is, then, in effect, like the artist's sign which, Brandt says, is of an "unambiguous nature, yet which cannot be interpreted without the sign itself disappearing."[2]

Clothes are not mangled in the pawnbroker's shop, and an investigation of the fact would render the sign meaningless. But it is not meaningless, because it indicates faith in the idea that clothes are mangled somewhere. Similarly, there is no substance behind the signs and pictures of art, but the signs and pictures are still valid if they indicate faith in the idea that the substance they represent does, in fact, exist somewhere. In order that the sign not disappear, "It is necessary that the audience be at the same time a congregation in the sense that it is at home in the poet's own language."[3] When the audience is "at home in the poet's own language," its attention is drawn,

1. "Et Essay om Karen Blixen," *Heretica,* VI (1953), no. 3, p. 300.
2. Ibid., p. 301.
3. Ibid.

it would seem, to a point beyond the language itself, to the possibility behind the signboard—to the blank page.

Isak Dinesen sees the artist's relation to his audience, says Brandt, as "a dialogue before a raised curtain out towards the people."[4] The people know that the stage is the pawnbroker's shop and that the play is the painted sign in the window. They do not expect the stage to contain what the play advertises. What the people demand is that the play advertise a possibility which they can believe to exist beyond the stage.

After Charlie Despard has concluded his lengthy remarks on the relationship between the artist and the public, Aeneas Snell tells him a story about a young prince who poses as a beggar to learn more about his people, only to discover that a real beggar, who is his double, is reaping a strange benefit from the prince's activities. The upshot of the story is that the beggar convinces the prince that the prince's duty is to play his assigned role, the performance of which, if done with integrity, will add to the greater glory of the beggar whom the people will mistake for the prince in disguise. It is an old story and a variation of one of Isak Dinesen's favorite themes: the relationship between master and slave and the necessity of one for the existence of the other. As the beggar in the story says: "My master, you and I, the rich and the poor of this world, are two locked caskets, of which each contains the key to the other."

This is the third time in the story that Fath, the beggar, uses the locked caskets metaphor. The first time he uses it, he is referring to life and death; the second time, to man and woman. On the principle of paradox which Isak Dinesen has established as the basis of interdependence, it can reasonably be deduced that artist and public—like life and death, man and woman, rich and poor—"are two locked caskets, of which each contains the key to the other." Each comes into being and acquires meaning only because of the presence of the other. And, like all paradoxes, they are resolved at that

4. Ibid., p. 301.

point just beyond the work of art wherein lies the magic of reconciliation—the blank page.

The concept of interdependence is one of Isak Dinesen's most fundamental and far-reaching attitudes towards both life and art. We have observed its importance in the relationship between God and artist, pride and humility, reality and dream, truth and mask, Logos and Mythos; and we have seen it offered as a clue to the understanding of the paradoxes of life and death, man and woman, rich and poor, artist and public. In the next chapter we shall see how interdependence culminates in reconciliation—that grand effect to which Isak Dinesen insists all art should, and great art does, aspire. Its underlying principle is best expressed in the words of Baron Brackel in "The Old Chevalier" (SGT): "to love, or cherish, the pride of your partner, or of your adversary, as you will define it, as highly or higher than your own."

Erik Johannesson recounts a little fireside talk given some years ago by Isak Dinesen in which she expressed her "faith in the importance of interaction and her conviction about the great riches and unlimited possibilities that are contained in the correspondence and interplay of two dissimilar entities."[5] He goes on to note how frequently the theme of interdependence runs through her tales, but he warns elsewhere that "as such it by no means offers a solution to the problem of life; rather it simply invites its own acceptance as the only real and genuine principle of order in human existence."[6] It is an attempt, he says, "to preserve the tension of opposites which gives order, harmony and value to human relations."[7] His warning is an important reminder to the reader that art is not an answer to the mystery of existence but a restatement of that mystery. The locked caskets remain locked.

---

5. "Isak Dinesen, Soren Kierkegaard, and the Present Age," *Books Abroad,* XXXV (1962)), no. 1, p. 22.

6. *The World of Isak Dinesen* (Seattle,), p. 113.

7. "Isak Dinesen, Soren Kierkegaard, and the Present Age," p. 23.

13

RECONCILIATION

Isak Dinesen was fond of quoting a Professor Zartmann who said that art actually is a higher degree of kindness.[1] After noting some of the demands which she expects the artist to make on the public, we may have difficulty understanding such treatment as kindness. It is a question of maneuvering the audience into a state of submissive gratitude much like the state in which Job finds himself at the end of his story. Such gratitude is a part of the reconciliation of opposites which Isak Dinesen considers the ultimate effect of art, and which justifies its rigorous demands. "The witty yet profound treatment of artist and his public in terms of God and Job," says Louise Bogan, "sums up . . . one problem of reconciliation"[2]—the problem, as I see it, of getting the public to accept its treatment as kindness.

Acceptance, like faith, precedes reconciliation—just as one embraces his destiny before he knows what it will be. Part of the purpose of Isak Dinesen's Job analogy is, I think, to impress upon the audience the necessity of accepting its treatment before it can move on to the reconciliation of the

---

1. Jørgen Gustava Brandt, "Et Essay om Karen Blixen," *Heretica*, VI (1953), no. 2, p. 213.

2. "Isak Dinesen," in *Selected Criticism* (New York, 1955), p. 233.

blank page. The way that acceptance and reconciliation inter-
act is described by Charlie Despard in "A Consolatory Tale"
(WT). He continues to speak in terms of God and Job, but
he has made clear to his listener, Aeneas Snell, that he is
really talking about the artist and the public.

"... in the end the two are reconciled; it is good to read about.
For the Lord in the whirlwind pleads the defense of the artist, and
of the artist only. He blows up the moral scruples and the moral
sufferings of his public; he does not attempt to justify his show
by any argument on right and wrong. 'Wilt thou disannul my
judgement?' asks the Lord. 'Knowest thou the ordinances of
heaven? Hast thou walked in the search of the depth? Canst thou
lift up thy voice to the clouds? Canst thou bind the sweet influence
of the Pleiades?' Yes, he speaks about the horrors and abomina-
tions of existence, and airily asks his public if they, too, will
play with them as with a bird, and let their young persons do the
same. And Job indeed is the ideal public. Who amongst us will
ever again find a public like that? Before such arguments he
bows his head and forgoes his grievance; he sees that he is better
off, and safer, in the hands of the artist than with any other power
of the world, and he admits that he has uttered what he understood not."

When the audience forgoes its grievance and sees that
it is better off, and safer, in the hands of the artist than with
any other power of the world, then it is ready, it seems, for
the moment of reconciliation. To lead the audience to this
point, the artist must counter its questions with overwhelming
evidence of his own greater right to question. God answers
Job by asking questions which makes Job's questions seem
trivial. This is what the artist does to the public; he convinces
it of the foolishness of its own questions and the absurdity
of wanting answers to them. He torments, baffles, maddens,
and surprises, but he never misleads. There is unremitting
honesty in his answers, but he answers his public the way
God anwers Job, "not logically but lyrically, in a series of
lyrical exaltations of His Creation. It is the artist's justifica-
tion of his work."[3] Instead of a logical answer, the artist seeks

---

3. Robert Langbaum, *The Gayety of Vision* (New York, 1956), p. 12.

to connect, to deepen the meaning of things in such a way as to surprise the reader "as he himself was one day surprised."[4]

The old artist in "Copenhagen Season" (LT) says: "For what is the end of all higher education? Regained naiveté." This is the reward of the artist's kindness to the public. "Our purpose, as we see it, is one thing," says Robert Langbaum in explanation of the old artist's remark, "and as the artist or God sees it quite another. . . . It is for reflecting creatures to know what your purpose is, to be as sure of it as are the wild animals who act on instinct. This is the sense in which art restores us to the connection with the absolute that we had in a state of nature, the sense in which 'regained naiveté' is . . . the end of our highest education."[5]

The regaining of naiveté is a regaining of the "lost unity of perception through an expansion of consciousness."[6] There can be no expansion of consciousness if the component parts of a work of art exist only to deceive. Where this is so, the individual parts have function without meaning, and all interest in them is lost once the final effect has been achieved. If the adventure turns out to have been a dream, or a boy a girl—and this is done with no purpose other than to mislead us—we feel cheated. But if such reversals deepen the meaning of both adventure and dream, boy and girl—by directing our attention to something beyond them—we feel rewarded. We have more, not less, than we started with. It is this "more" that I think Isak Dinesen means by reconciliation.

According to the romantic version, the paradox that regained Eden is superior to lost Eden is interpreted to mean that our return will be heightened by a knowledge of the loss engendered by the Fall and an increase in our appreciation of what we are regaining.[7] It is, I think, what Langbaum calls

---

4. Hanne Marie and Werner Svendsen, *Geschichte der dänischen Literatur* (Copenhagen, 1964), p. 478.

5. Langbaum, p. 12.

6. Ibid., p. 52.

7. Ibid.

elsewhere a "reconciling of the knowledge of life with the praise of it."[8] Such a reconciling demands that the audience must feel this sense of increase, this "more," as a part of the final effect. The valet in "The Deluge at Norderney" (SGT) may masquerade as a cardinal, and Miss Nat-og-Dag may be overwhelmed at his audacity; but before the story is over both she and the reader know that this masquerade is a bold and ingenious stroke that increases tremendously the effect of the story. The shock of this revelation lifts the reader to a point beyond the story from which he reviews all that has gone on in the story with a wider perspective. His awareness has been literally heightened, and he is surprised as the artist "himself was one day surprised."

This surprise is the awareness, on the part of both artist and audience, of the harmony that exists in things that are apparently opposite, together with the conviction that there is nothing irrelevant in the universe. If the work of art is successful, it will convey intact the sense of the unity and necessity of all things in such a way that the audience will recognize and accept the truth of this unity and necessity without asking why it is so or why it must be so. In fact, if harmony has been achieved and transmitted through the work of art, the audience will feel that such harmony is right and proper and is itself the answer to the seeming diversity and whim of isolated experiences. It will understand that "everything, even the pain and the evil, is esthetically necessary."[9]

Adam in "Sorrow-Acre" (WT) comes to perceive the unity and necessity behind the apparent chaos. "He saw the ways of life, he thought, as a twined and tangled design, complicated and mazy; it was not given him or any mortal to command or control it. Life and death, happiness and woe, the past and the present, were interlaced within the pattern. Yet to the initiated it might be read as easily as our ciphers—

8. Ibid., p. 3.
9. Ibid., p. 12.

which to the savage must seem confused and incomprehensible—will be read by the schoolboy. And out of the contrasting elements concord rose." Perhaps the word *balance* best describes what people respond to innately once they sense its presence in art. Jørgen Gustava Brandt says that Isak Dinesen does not seek a "compromise or solution for the sufferings and troubles of this world, but to find the great balance in all relations, that tension which one might call the symposion of existence, an art of life which is related to the rope-dancer's or to that of the Ecclesiastes."[10]

Balance is not necessarily achieved by presenting both sides in the work of art. The half is still better than the whole, but the other half must be implicit in the first half. The audience must be led to infer the missing half, for it is on the basis of this inference that it will make its judgment. It is a bad piece of art, says Charlie Despard in "A Consolatory Tale," in which the audience sees nothing, yet can still say, " 'Yet all that is I see.' "[11] Balance is struck only when the audience can perceive "the whole in the one-sidedness and the one-sidedness in the whole."[12] The Russian general in "The Invincible Slave-Owners" (WT) says that if we see a pair of lovers on the dance floor, we can assume the hayloft. If, however, we are told that the dance floor is the whole story, we become skeptical—and make our assumptions anyway.

However it is given to us, balance must be present in a work of art, it seems, before we can respond to it. We know that balance has been achieved once we see that opposites are interdependent. Out of this interdependence arises a concord that makes alternatives unimaginable. Once we have reached this point, we have arrived at the moment of reconciliation—the blank page. This is the moment in which the

---

10. "Et Essay om Karen Blixen," p. 209.

11. Also Gertrude's speech to Hamlet (*Hamlet,* act III, scene 4) when she cannot see the ghost of the dead king which Hamlet sees plainly. The use of this speech suggests that the fault may lie as easily in the audience as in the work of art.

12. Brandt, "Et Essay om Karen Blixen," *Heretica* VI (1953), no. 3, p. 307.

half that we have been given unites with the half which we can project, and question and answer become one. This is the point of the story "The Blank Page" (LT). The anonymous, unstained square of bridal linen hangs in bold contrast to the labeled, stained squares around it; but both the empty canvas and its opposites become parts of the same whole in the gallery of the cloister, under the royal crest. For it is the unstained piece of wedding sheet that gives meaning to the stained squares, and they which give it its peculiar prominence. In the end silence speaks, and "silence is the absolute. The story transforms human purposes into the divine purpose."[13]

Brandt calls Isak Dinesen "the poet of reconciliation—reconciliation with the world, life, existence, God—reconciliation through the total subjugation . . . the proudest form of subjugation."[14] Such subjugation comes through the audience's acceptance of the artist's treatment of it as "a higher degree of kindness." "When the listener has got ears to hear with," says Brandt, "he hears a voice that treats him the way God treats Job and requires that he recognize and love the world's order as himself and God higher than himself."[15] Such is the response to the artist and his art that Isak Dinesen expects from the audience.

Although Isak Dinesen makes it clear that reality and art are never to be confused—they, too, are locked caskets—she makes it equally clear, I think, that life without art can be confusing and narrow. Reality can grind us down and force us to reluctant and unsatisfying acceptances and compromises that leave us drained and unhappy, whereas art can lift us up and seduce us into an eager and willing acceptance of life's conditions in a joyful recognition of their necessity. Such is the sublime reconciliation of their necessity. Such is the sublime reconciliation to destiny which art achieves in contrast to what Baron von Brackel in "The Old Chevalier"

---

13. Langbaum, p. 12.
14. Brandt, no. 3, p. 303.
15. Ibid.

(SGT) calls "the dreadful reconciliation to fate which life works upon us when it gets time to impress us drop by drop." Art and reality are balanced and interdependent, but it is important to remember that this is a passive relationship. Each helps the audience to confront the other, not to change the other.

The trouble with talking in terms of art reconciling one with reality or reality reconciling one with art is that it suggests a separation, in time or experience, which is essentially false. One does not have to follow the other or be experienced separately from the other. Like dancers, they operate independently, yet interdependently, to achieve the dance. As partner, one cannot really exist without the other, and it is the effect that both together produce that takes place ideally in the mind of the audience. The reconciliation that occurs is not *with* reality or *with* art, but *between* reality and art. It is a spiritual state, which, like the dance, is something beyond the elements involved in achieving it—something which grows out of the interdependence of reality and art, but which transcends both.

It is the rebellious tendency of romanticism to posit art at the extreme opposite of existing concepts of sensually perceptible reality. Isak Dinesen is merely reaffirming this tendency by constantly dealing in terms of paradox and resolution, in terms of thesis, antithesis, and synthesis. Nowhere are such terms more applicable or more appropriate, it seems, than in this ultimate achievement of art—to join with reality in a reconciliation that transcends both. In her own life and art Isak Dinesen repeatedly insisted on an equal acquaintance with art and reality for this very reason, and not on an understanding of one by means of the other.

Logos and Mythos, creation and art, tragedy and comedy, reality and mask, artist and audience. God and man—the list is endless—all are subsumed in a higher essence which we cannot anticipate but in which we must believe. Isak Dinesen asks us first to believe—that creation and art have meaning, that we are safe in the hands of God and the artist, that reconciliation is possible and desirable—and then submit willingly, on the basis of that belief, to destiny as we discover it in reality and art.

BIBLIOGRAPHY

Primary material (in order of publication)

Dinesen, Isak. *Seven Gothic Tales.* New York, 1934.

_____. *Out of Africa.* New York, 1938.

_____. *Winter's Tales.* New York, 1942.

_____. *Last Tales.* New York, 1957.

_____. *Anecdotes of Destiny.* New York, 1958.

_____. *Shadows on the Grass.* New York, 1961.

_____. *Ehrengard.* New York, 1963.

Secondary material

Biography

Migel, Parmenia. *Titania: The Biography of Isak Dinesen.* New York, 1967.

Criticism and Related Commentary

Andersen, Hans. "Om Karen Blixen," *Almanak,* I (1967), no. 6, 10-11.

Antonini, Giacomo. "I Racconti Bizzari di Isak Dinesen," *La Fiera Letteraria* (22 June 1958), pp. 7-8.

Arendt, Hannah. "Isak Dinesen: 1885-1962," *New Yorker* (9 November 1968), pp. 223-236.

Blixen-Finecke, Bror von. *African Hunter*. Translated from the Swedish by F. H. Lyon. New York, 1938.

Bogan, Louise. "Isak Dinesen," in *Selected Criticism* (New York, 1955), pp. 231-234.

Brandes, Georg. *The Romantic School in Germany*. Vol. II of *Main Currents in Nineteenth Century Literature*. New York, 1902.

Brandt, Jørgen Gustava. "Et Essay om Karen Blixen," *Heretica,* VI (1953), no. 2, 200-223.

_____. "Et Essay om Karen Blixen," *Heretica,* VI (1953), no. 3, 300-320.

Brix, Hans. *Karen Blixens Eventyr*. Copenhagen, 1949.

_____. "Sandhedens Haevn Til Isak Dinesen: "Vejene omkring Pisa,' et Eventyr af Karen Blixen," Analyser og Problemer, VI (Copenhagen, 1950), 286-306.

Cate, Curtis. "Isak Dinesen: The Scheherazade of Our Times," *Cornhill Magazine* (Winter 1959-60), pp. 120-137.

_____. "Isak Dinesen," *Atlantic Monthly* (December, 1959), pp. 151-155.

Claudi, Jørgen. *Contemporary Danish Authors*. (Copenhagen, 1952), pp. 109-114.

Davenport, John. "A Noble Pride: The Art of Karen Blixen." *Twentieth Century* (March 1956), pp. 264-274.

Dinesen, Isak. (Memorial anthology), New York, 1964. Prints contributions in English, French, and German, but omits Danish contributions except for articles in English by Thomas Dinesen and Clara Svendsen. These omitted articles are included in *Karen Blixen,* a memorial anthology with prose and verse by European,

American, and African contributors, translated into Danish and edited by Clara Svendsen and Ole Wivel (Copenhagen, 1962).

Elling, Christian. "Karen Blixen," in *Danske Digtere i det Tyvende Aarhundrede,* ed. Ernst Frandsen and Niels Kaas Johansen (Copenhagen, 1951), pp. 521-555.

Fichte, Johann Gottlieb. "The Vocation of Man," trans. William Smith, in *The European Philosophers from Descartes to Nietzsche.* Ed. Monroe C. Beardsley (New York, 1960), pp. 490-531.

Frandsen, Ernst. "Udsigt over et halvt Aarhundrede," in *Danske Digtere i det Tyvende Aarhundrede.* Ed. Ernst Frandsen and Niels Kaas Johansen (Copenhagen, 1951), pp. 5-32.

Grandjean, Louis E. *Blixens Animus.* Copenhagen, 1957.

Hannah, Donald. *'Isak Dinesen' and Karen Blixen: The Mask and the Reality.* London, 1971.

——————. "In Memoriam Karen Blixen," *Sewanee Review,* LXXI, no. 4 (Autumn 1963), 585-604.

Hegel, Georg Wilhelm Friedrich. From "The Phenomenology of Mind," trans. J. B. Baillie, in *The Modern Tradition: Backgrounds of Modern Literature.* Ed. Richard Ellman and Charles Feidelson, Jr. (New York, 1965), pp. 739-741.

Henriksen, Aage. *Det Guddommelige Barn og Andre Essays om Karen Blixen.* Copenhagen, 1965.

——————. *Guder og galgefugle: To essays om Karen Blixen.* Oslo, 1956.

Johannesson, Eric O. "Isak Dinesen, Søren Kierkegaard, and the Present Age," *Books Abroad,* XXXV (1962), no. 1, 20-24.

——————. *The World of Isak Dinesen.* Seattle, 1961.

Kristensen, Tom. "Syv fantastiske Fortaellinger," *Mellem Krigene* (Copenhagen, 1946), pp. 134-140.

Langbaum, Robert. *The Gayety of Vision: A Study of the Art of Isak Dinesen.* New York, 1965.

Linnemann, Willy-August, *Bogen om det skjulte Ansigt.* Copenhagen, 1958.

Madsen, Børge G. "Isak Dinesen, a Modern Aristocrat," *American-Scandinavian Review* (Winter 1953), pp. 328-332.

Mitchell, P. M. *A History of Danish Literature* (Copenhagen, 1957), pp. 275-278.

Nielsen, Harald. *Karen Blixen: En Studie i litteraer Mystik.* Copenhagen, 1956.

Poulsen, Kuno. "Karen Blixens gamle og nye Testamente," *Vindrosen,* X (1963), no. 5, 364-380.

Riisager, Vagn. *Karen Blixen.* Copenhagen, 1952.

Rosendahl, Johannes. *Karen Blixen: Fire Foredrag.* Copenhagen, 1957.

Schlegel, Friedrich. From "Lyceum of the Fine Arts," in *The Modern Tradition: Backgrounds of Modern Literature.* Trans. and ed. Richard Ellmann and Charles Feidelson, Jr. (New York, 1965), p. 739.

Stafford, Jean. "Isak Dinesen: Master Teller of Tales" (interview), *Horizon* (September 1959), pp. 111-112.

—————. "Lioness" (review of *Titania*), *New York Review* (18 January 1968).

Svendsen, Clara. "Karen Blixen som Maler," *Almanak,* I (1967), no. 6, 2-9.

Svendsen, Hanne Marie and Werner. *Geschichte der dänischen Literatur* (Copenhagen, 1964), pp. 478-480.

Van Doren, Mark. "The Eighth Gothic Tale (on *Out of Africa*)," *The Private Reader* (New York, 1942), pp. 277-281.

Vinding, Ole. "Karen Blixen og det gyldne snit," *Ord Och Bild* (Stockholm, 1958), no. 1, 47-52.

Vogt, Per. "Tilfellet Karen Blixen," *Tendenser Mot Tiden: Kuluressays og Portretter* (Oslo, 1946), pp. 123-139.

Walter, Eugene. "Isak Dinesen" (interview), *Paris Review* (Autumn 1956), pp. 43-59.

Walzel, Oskar. *German Romanticism.* New York, 1965.

Wernaer, Robert M. *Romanticism and the Romantic School in Germany.* New York, 1966.

Wescott, Glenway. "Isak Dinesen, the Storyteller," *Images of Truth* (New York and Evanston, 1962), chap. 6, p. 151.

_____. "Isak Dinesen Tells a Tale," *Harper's Magazine,* CCXX (March 1960), 67-72.

INDEX

129